POWER
HOUSE
PUBLISHING

ALEXANDRIA
VIRGINIA

BOOMER SELLS THE BUSINESS

A Step-by-Step Guide to Cashing Out & Living Large

FRANK FELKER | MARTY M FAHNCKE

Boomer Sells The Business Paperback Edition
A Step-By-Step Guide to Cashing Out and Living Large

by Frank Felker and Marty M. Fahncke

Published by:
Powerhouse Publishing
277 S Washington Street
Suite 210
Alexandria, Virginia 22314

info@powerhousepublishing.biz
703-473-8885

First paperback printing April 2025
Printed in the United States of America

Felker, Frank | Fahncke, Marty M.
Boomer Sells The Business,
A Step-By-Step Guide to Cashing Out and Living Large
1st paperback ed.

ISBN: 978-0-9994903-6-5

Disclaimer

The information provided in Boomer Sells The Business is for educational and informational purposes only. While we, the authors, have drawn upon our professional experiences and expertise to create this book, we make no guarantees or promises regarding the outcomes or results of implementing the strategies and suggestions discussed within these pages.

We are not attorneys, accountants, or financial planners. This book is not a substitute for professional advice. Before making any decisions or taking any actions based on the content of this book, we strongly recommend consulting with qualified professionals, including but not limited to attorneys, accountants, tax advisors, financial planners, and business consultants, who can address your specific circumstances and objectives.

The authors and publisher disclaim any liability for loss or damage resulting from the use or misuse of the information contained in this book. The responsibility for all decisions and actions rests solely with the reader. Your situation is unique, and the strategies outlined in this book may not apply to or suit your specific needs or circumstances.

The examples and case studies presented are illustrative and are not intended to represent or predict actual results. Past performance or success discussed in this book does not guarantee future outcomes.

By reading this book, you acknowledge and accept that you are responsible for your decisions and actions, and you agree to hold the authors and publisher harmless from any liability, loss, or harm that may result.

Table of Contents

INTRODUCTION: Now Is The Time

SECTION I: Top 10 Questions Owners Ask About Selling

SECTION II:
Six Reasons To Always Have Your Business in Sale-Ready Condition

SECTION III: Seven Steps to Sale-Ready Condition

SECTION IV: The Sale Process - 15 Steps to Your Exit

SECTION V: Financing

SECTION VI: Cashing Out and Living Large

Here's What to Do Next

Acknowledgments

Many people beyond Frank and Marty have contributed their wisdom and experience to this book, the Companion Workbook, and our Online MasterClass. While you will see their names mentioned throughout, we wanted to explicitly acknowledge their contributions here at the front of the book.

Douglas Wick
An expert in Business Operating Systems and a seasoned implementer of the Entrepreneurial Operating System® (EOS), Doug shared invaluable insights on how systematizing a business dramatically increases its value and transferability. Doug's concise, actionable guidance makes it clear why documenting processes, aligning teams, and creating accountability structures are essential steps in preparing a business for sale.

Douglas Wick
Strategic Advisor
Positioning Systems
dwick@positioningsystems.com

Jerome Myers
A nationally recognized authority on business exits and the author of Exit to Excellence, Jerome shared powerful insights into the emotional journey of stepping away from business ownership. Through his thoughtful perspective, Jerome helped illuminate why psychological preparation is just as essential as financial readiness. His reflections on identity, purpose, and post-exit reinvention bring much-needed depth to this book's final section. By highlighting the human side of selling a business, Jerome reminds us that true success comes not just from cashing out—but from moving forward with clarity and confidence.

Jerome Myers
Founder
Exit to Excellence
ExitToExcellence.com

Kelly Guinaugh

Founder and former owner of Interior Enhancement Group, Kelly Guinaugh, generously shared her firsthand experience preparing and successfully selling her high-end interior design business. Her story highlights the real-world challenges of letting go - emotionally and operationally - and the value of surrounding yourself with the right advisors. Kelly's disciplined approach to preparation, combined with her openness about the ups and downs of the process, brought authenticity and inspiration to this book. Her insights underscore a central truth: with intention and guidance, selling your business can be both profitable and deeply fulfilling.

Kelly Guinaugh
Enjoying Her Retirement

Alexis Grant

Alexis is a two-time founder who successfully exited both her content marketing agency and The Write Life, a site she bootstrapped into a six-figure asset. Drawing on the lessons learned from those sales, Alexis created They Got Acquired - a media company and resource hub that shines a light on small- and mid-sized business exits typically overlooked by mainstream outlets. By sharing real stories - including A Tale of Two Exits in our Introduction - insightful data, and practical tools, Alexis empowers founders to understand and navigate the complex process of selling a business with confidence and clarity.

Alexis Grant
Founder, They Got Acquired
https://TheyGotAcquired.com

Diana Gibb

With decades of experience guiding people through life's most difficult transitions, psychotherapist Diana Gibb helped us understand the emotional roadblocks that prevent many business owners from preparing for the sale of their business. Diana's insights into how fear, overwhelm, and a desire for simplicity can derail even the most successful entrepreneurs, brought a crucial dimension to this book. Her perspective reminded us that selling your business isn't just a financial transaction—it's a deeply personal journey, and emotional readiness is just as important as operational readiness.

Diana Gibb
Psychotherapist
LinkedIn.com/in/dianasgibb/

Mission Statement

Boomer Sells The Business is more than a book or a workbook. It's more than a checklist, webinar, or training program. Boomer Sells The Business is a Movement.

We are dedicated to empowering ALL small business owners, of all ages, everywhere in the world, to maximize the value of their businesses as they prepare for retirement - or for their next adventure! Our mission is to provide comprehensive, actionable strategies and expert guidance that ensure businesses are in optimal, sale-ready condition.

Through our publications, presentations, online courses, expert consultations, and community, we teach business owners how to navigate the complexities of selling their businesses, allowing them to secure their financial futures and enjoy the retirement they deserve.

Boomer Sells The Business is committed to addressing the unique challenges faced by mature business owners, ensuring that their hard work and legacy translate into a rewarding financial outcome and a fulfilling post-exit life.

Most importantly, we believe in fostering a community of informed, prepared, and confident business owners who can approach the sale of their business not as an end, but as a transition to new opportunities and financial security - and support each other on that journey.

Why You Need This Book

If you're like most business owners, you've poured years, if not decades, of your life into building a successful company. You've overcome challenges, navigated economic ups and downs, and developed a deep sense of pride in what you've built. However, we firmly believe that, whether you plan to sell your business next year, five years from now, or not at all, one truth remains: your business should always be in sale-ready condition.

Many business owners assume they'll have time to prepare when they're ready to sell, but reality doesn't always allow for careful planning. Sudden life events, market disruptions, or emotional burnout can force an unexpected sale. The difference between a well-prepared business and one that's unprepared can mean hundreds of thousands - or even millions - of dollars in lost valuation. This book was written to prevent that from happening to you.

The goal of Boomer Sells the Business is simple: to help you sell your business for the highest possible price to the optimal buyer, on your terms. Whether you plan to transition in the near future or years down the road, the steps outlined in this book will help you increase profitability, improve operational efficiency, and position your business as an attractive investment.

Six Reasons You Need This Book Now

1. Maximize Your Business's Value
A business that is prepared for sale is more valuable - plain and simple. Many owners overestimate what their business is worth, assuming that buyers will see its potential the way they do. But buyers don't purchase potential. They invest in proven profitability, strong financials, and systems that allow the business to run without you.

By following the strategies in this book, you will:

- Understand how buyers value businesses and what will make yours attractive.
- Identify ways to increase revenue, profit margins, and efficiency before a sale.
- Ensure you're not leaving money on the table when it's time to sell.

2. Protect Yourself Against the Unexpected

You may not be planning to sell your business today, but life has a way of changing our plans without notice. Divorce, illness, financial downturns, partner disputes, or simply exhaustion can suddenly put you in a position where selling is no longer optional, it's necessary.

If you wait until that moment to prepare, you'll be forced into a rushed sale, often at a fraction of the price your business could have commanded with proper preparation. Keeping your business sale-ready protects your financial future and gives you peace of mind, knowing you can sell under the right circumstances rather than being forced into a fire sale.

3. Improve Your Business, Even If You Don't Sell

Preparing your business for sale doesn't just benefit you when it's time to exit, it improves your company right now. The same strategies that make your business attractive to buyers also make it easier to operate, more profitable, efficient, and enjoyable to own.

Many business owners who follow the steps in this book discover that their newly optimized business is so much easier and more enjoyable to run that they decide to keep it longer. Wouldn't you rather own a business that runs smoothly, generates higher profits, and requires less of your daily involvement?

This book will help you:

- Reduce your workload while increasing profits.
- Eliminate inefficiencies and allow your business to run without you.
- Have the option to sell when the time is right, instead of being forced to sell under pressure.

4. Attract Strategic Investors and Growth Opportunities

Not every business transition is a full sale. Even if you're not ready to exit completely, keeping your business in sale-ready condition makes it attractive to:

- Strategic investors looking to acquire part of your company.

- Private equity firms seeking businesses with strong financials and leadership teams.

- Partnership opportunities that could scale your business beyond what you can achieve alone.

When your business is well-positioned, you control your future. Instead of scrambling for buyers, you may find that buyers come to you with opportunities you never expected.

5. Secure Your Legacy

For many entrepreneurs, their business is more than just a source of income, it's a legacy. Whether you plan to sell to an outside buyer, transfer ownership to employees, or pass the business to family members, a well-prepared business ensures a smooth and profitable transition.

A sale-ready business is a business with a future. If your company is dependent on you to function, it's not truly a business, it's a job. This book will help you implement the systems, processes, and leadership structure necessary for your company to thrive long after you exit.

6. Gain Peace of Mind and Financial Freedom

The ultimate goal of this book is to give you options, not obligations. Whether you decide to sell or keep running your business, the strategies here ensure that you:

- Have a valuable, sellable business at all times.

- Can step away without operations falling apart.

- Have financial security and control over your exit strategy.

Take Control of Your Exit, Before It's Too Late

Every year, business owners come to us too late, when they need to sell fast and have zero leverage to negotiate a strong deal. The result? They walk away with less than they could have.

By reading this book, you are taking control of your future now. Whether you plan to sell in six months or six years, these strategies will put you in the best possible position to:

- Sell for the highest possible price.
- Attract the right buyer.
- Exit on your terms.

You've built something valuable. Now it's time to make sure you get paid what it's worth.

How to Use This Book

This book follows a logical, step-by-step progression designed to teach you how to make your business more valuable, more attractive to buyers, and easier to sell.

Each section covers a key component of the sale process:

Understanding Why You Need a Sale-Ready Business
How to structure your business to be valuable and sellable at any time.

Preparing for a Sale
The foundational steps to increase profitability, streamline operations, and position your business for a premium valuation.

The Sale Process
A deep dive into the 15 steps of selling your business, from selecting your exit team to negotiating the deal and transitioning ownership.

Financing Options
A breakdown of the various ways buyers may finance the acquisition, including SBA loans, bank loans, seller financing, and earnouts.

Maximizing Your Exit
How to ensure a smooth sale, avoid common pitfalls, and walk away with the best possible deal.

By following the structure of this book, you will gain a clear understanding of each step in the process and avoid the costly mistakes that derail so many business sales.

To make the best use of this book, follow these simple guidelines:

1. Read The Entire Book First, Then Return to It for Reference
Some readers may choose to review the table of contents and then just jump directly to one or more areas of interest. We strongly recommend you not do that until you have read the entire book from cover to cover.

Beyond the educational "ah-ha" moments, timelines, case studies, and cited resources, what we really want you to take away from this book is a new perspective on your business and your future exit. That objective can only be achieved by a thorough reading of the full text. You can then come back to refresh your memory on specific points later.

2. Follow the Process in Order

Here's another great reason to read the whole book through: each step builds on the last. Understanding your valuation target, for example, is critical before you can confidently negotiate a deal. The better prepared you are in advance, the stronger your position will be when it's time to sell.

3. Apply What You Learn to Your Business

This book is not just about theory. Every section contains real-world advice, strategies, best practices, and case studies. As you read, take time to evaluate your own business through the lens of what you're learning. Ask yourself:

- Is my business structured to run without me?
- Are my financial records clear, organized, and ready for scrutiny?
- Have I identified my ideal buyer type?
- What steps can I take now to increase my valuation over the next few years?

By treating this book as a working guide rather than passive reading material, you'll put yourself in the best position to sell for top dollar.

How This Book Works with the Companion Workbook

While this book provides the strategic roadmap, the Boomer Sells The Business Workbook is your interactive planning tool.

The Primary Book (this book) will:

- Give you the why and how behind every step of selling a business.
- Offer real-world examples & case studies to illustrate key concepts.
- Provide expert insights from a wide range of experienced business experts, as well as experienced business buyers, and successful business sellers.

The Companion Workbook will:

- Provide step-by-step exercises and checklists to apply the concepts to your business.

- Help you document key decisions and track your progress.

- Include fillable worksheets that allow you to assess your valuation, identify buyer types, and prepare marketing materials.

Together, the book and the workbook create a complete system for successfully preparing and selling your business. The workbook ensures you take action on the principles outlined in this book, helping you turn knowledge into results.

Commit to the Process and Take Action

Selling your business for the highest possible price to the optimal buyer doesn't happen by chance. It requires planning, preparation, and execution. Boomer Sells The Business is designed to give you a clear, no-nonsense approach to getting your business sale-ready.

The sooner you start, the more options you'll have when the time comes to sell. Use this book, work through the companion workbook, and begin preparing today, so that when the time comes you'll be in control of the process, not at the mercy of it.

About The Authors

About Frank Felker

The bestselling author of six books on marketing, sales, and business ownership, Frank's 50+ years of entrepreneurial experience have run the gamut from home-based and storefront businesses to the founding of a tech start-up where he raised over $3 million in seed and early-stage venture capital and became the Chairman and CEO of a publicly-traded firm.

Today he focuses on sharing what he has learned about starting and growing successful businesses through his podcast, Radio Free Enterprise, his 24/7 streaming video channel, Small Biz School TV, and the Frank Felker School of Business, which counts over 26,000 business owners from 170 countries as students.

You can connect with Frank on every social media platform, at frankfelker.com, or by email at frank@boomersellsthebusiness.com

About Marty M. Fahncke

Marty M. Fahncke is a seasoned, world-class marketer with over 35 years of experience in growing & scaling businesses, and over 25 years of experience in Mergers and Acquisitions.

Marty has helped businesses scale to over $1 billion in revenue and executed over $450 million in Mergers and Acquisitions transactions.

Marty offers his expertise as an M&A Advisor, assisting business owners in the successful process of selling or acquiring businesses. He knows that buying or selling a business can be a time-consuming, stressful, and emotional experience. But with expert guidance from Marty and the team from Westbound Road, it can also be rewarding and lucrative.

You can connect with Marty on every social media platform, at WestboundRoad.com, or by email at marty@boomersellsthebusiness.com

How Marty and Frank Came to Write This Book Together

In 2004, Frank Felker started the Radio Free Enterprise podcast. In 2006, a friend of Frank's told him about a company called Conference Call University, run by a guy named Marty M. Fahncke. Frank reached out to Marty to ask him a few questions, and what resulted was Marty's very first guest appearance on a podcast.

Since then, both Marty and Frank have done scores of podcast interviews including two more appearances by Marty on Radio Free Enterprise. After one such interview in 2024, Frank told Marty about an idea he had for a book titled, Boomer Sells The Business.

The rest, as they say, is history.

Introduction: Now Is The Time

Why So Few Owners
Sell Their Businesses

Your business is more than just a source of income. It's a reflection of your personal identity, your hard work, your problem-solving abilities, and the sacrifices you've made all along the way. That's why, when the idea of selling your business enters the conversation, you may sense some emotional resistance.

We get it.

That emotional reaction is perhaps the biggest reason so few business owners ever sell their businesses—even though a successful sale could possibly provide them with financial security for the rest of their lives. Instead, many simply walk away, shut down, or hold on too long, only to either "die at their desk" or sell at a fraction of what their business could have been worth.

A survey of business owners nearing retirement found that 75% planned to sell their businesses within the next decade. But, according to hard market data, only 20% of business owners actually succeed in selling when the time comes. What happened to the rest? Some never prepared. Some waited too long. And many never even explored the possibility because they felt overwhelmed, unprepared, or frightened by the process.

If any of that sounds familiar, you're in the right place.

Selling Your Business Is a Major Life Transition

It's not just about numbers on a balance sheet. Selling your business is one of the most significant transitions of your life.

Think about it: What happens when your daily routine no longer revolves around the company you built? Who are you once you're no longer "the boss"?

We spoke with Diana Gibb, a psychotherapist who has worked extensively with people navigating major life changes. She confirmed something we've seen time and again—the psychological and emotional impacts of selling a business are just as important to prepare for as the financial ramifications.

Diana pointed out that as people approach major transitions, like retirement, they often have an existential instinct to simplify, rather than further complicate, their lives. This instinct may lead them to ignore or postpone complex and difficult decisions, including selling their business. There's just one problem with that instinct: Avoidance doesn't make the complexity disappear. It only makes selling harder and less rewarding when the time comes.

We also spoke with Jerome Myers, an expert on business exits and the author of Exit to Excellence. Jerome emphasized how most business owners get trapped in the "operator" mindset, running the day-to-day operations but never truly stepping into the role of an entrepreneur who can sell, transition, and move on profitably.

The solution? Treat the sale of your business like the biggest business opportunity you've ever been offered.

Preparing for a Sale Maximizes Your Financial Future

If you're going to sell your business, you want to do it on your terms, at the right time, and for the highest possible price to the optimal buyer. But that doesn't happen by accident.

A successful business sale requires careful planning, strategic positioning, and a clear understanding of what buyers are looking for.

Here's what we know for sure:

- Businesses that are sale-ready at all times command higher valuations.
- The sooner you start preparing, the more control you have over the process.
- Avoiding the sale decision won't make it go away, and by preparing now you will ensure that you get the best outcome when the time comes.

Whether you plan to sell in one year, three years, or ten years, the strategies in this book will help you maximize the value of your business while giving you the freedom to decide when and how you transition.

Why We Wrote This Book

We have both spent our adult lives building and selling businesses, helping entrepreneurs, and watching too many of our fellow business owners leave money on the table when the time came to sell because they didn't prepare in advance.

That's why we wrote Boomer Sells The Business.

This book is a step-by-step guide to preparing your business for sale, navigating the sale process, and ultimately achieving the financial reward and peace of mind you deserve.

If you've ever felt like:

- You don't even know where to start when it comes to selling your business
- You're unsure how much your business is worth—or how to increase that number
- You're overwhelmed by the idea of making a mistake that costs you time and money
- You're afraid of what your life will look like after the sale

Then this book was written for you.

Start Today, With This Book as Your Guide

- **Take it one step at a time.** You don't need to know - or do - everything at once. Each chapter builds on the previous one.

- **Use the Companion Workbook.** The Boomer Sells The Business Workbook is a practical tool that helps you apply the strategies in this book to your business, step by step.

- **Start now.** As the saying goes, "The best time to plant a tree was 20 years ago. The second-best time is today." The same is true for preparing your business for sale. The earlier you start, the more options you'll have.

This book isn't about forcing you to sell your business before you're ready. It's about giving you the knowledge, confidence, and strategies to sell on your terms, when the time is right for you.

A Tale of Two Exits

If the entire mission of Boomer Sells The Business could be boiled down to two words, they would be Prepare Now.

Time and again throughout this book, the Companion Workbook, our online MasterClass, and all of our social media posts and live presentations, you will hear us emphasize the critical nature of the mindset and actions required to get your business to sale-ready condition, and keep it there - even if you have no plans to sell your business now or in the near future.

With that in mind, we want to open with a story which compares two business owners looking to sell similar businesses. One owner had previously taken the steps necessary to bring his business to sale-ready condition and keep it there, while the other had not. Our thanks to Alexis Grant and her team at TheyGotAcquired.com for sharing this instructive tale. We have taken a bit of editorial license (adding "Steve's" story) in order to better make our point.

Why Preparation Makes All the Difference

Picture two different business founders, running successful businesses across the street from each other, both deciding it was time to sell around the same time. Because of the way they each approached the process, the results they achieved couldn't have been more different.

The first owner, let's call him "Steve," had built a solid company with recurring revenue, a loyal customer base, and a strong team. But when an unexpected opportunity to sell presented itself, he wasn't ready. His company was not in sale-ready condition.

His financial statements were outdated and inaccurate. His valuation target was way out of line with the marketplace. He had not created or implemented a systematic owner exit plan. He hadn't considered what type of buyer would be best for his customers and employees going forward. And most of the company's internal knowledge lived inside his head, not in documented systems or processes.

As the due diligence process dragged on, the buyer's interest cooled, and ultimately the deal fell through. Steve went back to work empty handed, frustrated, and beginning to feel a little burned out, uncertain whether he'd get another shot at selling his business.

Contrast that with the experience of Ryan Doyle and his co-founder, who successfully sold their business, Arrows, to another company in their same business space. They didn't wait until the last minute to get their house in order. Instead, they spent time cleaning up their books, documenting processes, and creating internal dashboards that gave buyers full visibility into the health of the business well ahead of time. Their preparation paid off, not only did they receive multiple offers, but they were also able to negotiate a higher valuation because buyers saw a company that was both well-run and ready to scale.

In an interview with They Got Acquired, Ryan said, "One of the biggest advantages we had going into the sale process was how prepared we were. Buyers could see everything clearly, and that gave them confidence - not just in the business, but in us as operators."

If you've been telling yourself, "I'll get ready when I'm ready to sell," Ryan's story - and Steve's - should give you pause. Deals don't wait, and opportunities rarely show up on a schedule. And, on the negative side, the Five Ds and a B (Divorce, Disease, Death, Debt, Disagreements, and Burnout) can jump up and bite you unexpectedly at any time. If you want to sell your business for the highest possible price to the optimal buyer - at any point in the future - the time to start preparing is now.

Choosing the Right Path
to Sell Your Business

When it comes time to sell your business, one of the most important decisions you'll make is how to go about it. Should you try to sell it yourself? Should you hire a business broker? Or would working with an acquisitions advisor provide the best outcome?

Each option has advantages and disadvantages, and which one is right for you depends on the size of your business, your timeline, your personal comfort level, and your financial goals. Let's examine each approach so you can make an informed decision.

Option 1: Do-It-Yourself (DIY) - The Temptation to Go It Alone

It's natural to consider selling your business yourself, especially if you already have a potential buyer in hand or want to avoid paying a commission. But just because you can doesn't mean you should.

Why Owners Consider DIY

- **Save on Commission Fees:** The most common motivation is to avoid paying an intermediary a percentage of the sale.

- **Trust in Known Buyers:** Some owners already have a buyer in mind - a competitor, employee, or customer - who has expressed interest.

- **Confidence in Negotiation Skills:** Especially for serial entrepreneurs, there's often a sense that they know enough to manage the process.

How DIY Can Backfire

- **Undervaluation:** You may accept a lower price without realizing it. A single interested buyer rarely generates the highest offer. Multiple buyers competing to acquire your business bid-up the highest price.

- **Legal and Structural Mistakes:** Without expert help, you could mishandle valuation, taxes, deal structure, or legal terms—errors that can cost you dearly.

- **Lack of Competitive Offers:** Experienced intermediaries bring multiple buyers to the table, creating competition and driving up your sale price.

If you've never sold a business before, trying to do it yourself can be like rebuilding a car engine with no experience. You might get it running, but it's unlikely to perform well, and you could do significant damage along the way.

Option 2: Hiring a Business Broker - The Local Guide

Business brokers typically specialize in selling smaller, local, or "Main Street" businesses - restaurants, medical practices, home service contractors, and other enterprises valued under a couple million dollars.

When a Broker Might Be the Right Fit

- **Your Business Is Local:** A broker with knowledge of your area and industry niche can bring in qualified local buyers.

- **You're in a Smaller Revenue Bracket:** If your business is worth under $2 million, a broker may be the best choice.

- **You Need Help, But Not a Long-Term Consultant:** Brokers are transactional - they jump in when you're ready to sell and stay to the end of the deal.

Potential Drawbacks of Using a Business Broker

- **Inconsistent Quality:** The business brokerage industry is largely unregulated, and quality varies dramatically from one broker to the next. Some lack sufficient experience or expertise.

- **Low Close Rates:** According to the International Business Brokers Association, only 15–20% of businesses listed with brokers actually sell.

- **Limited Buyer Networks:** Many brokers rely on local buyers and listing websites. If your business could command interest beyond your region, you may be leaving money on the table.

- **The Transactional Nature of Brokers:** Because business brokers are only in the picture while your business is being marketed, they are likely to take a more "transactional" approach to your deal, only bringing you cash or SBA deals that will allow them to more quickly collect their commission and move on to the next transaction. This approach, however, may cause them to overlook more complicated, but potentially more lucrative, deals with creative financing or other less well-known funding components.

Due diligence is essential. Before signing with any broker, ask for references - including from clients whose businesses did not sell. Find out why deals failed and whether the issue was with the broker or the business itself.

Option 3: Working with an Acquisitions Advisor: Strategic, Hands-On Support

An acquisitions advisor offers a more comprehensive, long-term approach, ideal for business owners seeking to sell for $2 million or more. Advisors aren't just matchmakers; they help you prepare your business for sale well in advance and work with you every step of the way.

When to Choose an Acquisitions Advisor

- **Your Business Has Strong Revenue or Growth Potential:** If you're aiming for a sale price between $2 million and $25 million, an acquisitions advisor can help you command top dollar.

- **You Want Strategic Guidance:** Advisors can engage with you months or years before the sale to help improve operations, financials, and presentation - making your business more attractive to buyers.

- **You're Open to Creative Deal Structures:** Advisors often help construct deals that include earnouts, seller financing, and other tools that can benefit both parties.

- **You Need a Broader Network:** Advisors have access to national and international buyers, private equity firms, rollup buyers, and strategic investors.

What to Expect When Working with an Acquisitions Advisor

- **Upfront Consulting Fees:** Since advisors often work with you over the course of months or years before the sale, some charge initial fees in addition to a success fee at closing.

- **More Creative, Flexible Compensation Structures:** Unlike brokers, who require full commission in cash at closing, advisors may structure their own compensation to align with the deal, ensuring the best outcome for both seller and buyer.

In short, an acquisitions advisor is a good choice if you want a trusted partner who will guide you through the process, help maximize the value of your business, and ensure a smoother transition for all involved.

Bonus: What About Investment Bankers?

If your company is valued north of $25 million, you may be in investment banker territory. These professionals provide high-level services similar to acquisitions advisors but are equipped to manage even larger, more complex transactions. However, their fees are significantly higher, and they're rarely appropriate for deals under $20–25 million.

Choosing the Right Path for You

Here's a simple way to think about your options:

- **DIY:** Only advisable if you've sold multiple businesses before and know exactly what you're doing - or if the sale is extremely small and simple.

- **Business Broker:** Best for smaller, local businesses (under $2 million in value) where access to local buyers is key.

- **Acquisitions Advisor:** Ideal for businesses valued at $2 million to $25 million, where strategic preparation, multiple buyer options, and deal structure creativity are critical.

Whichever path you choose, remember this: You will only sell this business once. Enlisting expert help can be the key difference between walking away disappointed and securing the financial freedom you've spent a lifetime building.

Your Exit Team and Their Roles

When it comes time to sell your business, going it alone isn't just risky - it can be costly. One of the smartest moves you can make is to assemble a trusted team of professionals who specialize in business acquisitions. Together, they'll guide you through the process, help you avoid expensive mistakes, and maximize the value of your sale.

At a minimum, your Exit Team should include three core professionals:

- A Mergers and Acquisitions (M&A) attorney

- A Tax Advisor

- A Business Broker or Acquisitions Advisor

Each plays a distinct and critical role in ensuring your sale proceeds smoothly and profitably.

The M&A Attorney:
Your Legal Guardian (Not Your Negotiator)

You must work with an attorney who has direct experience in mergers and acquisitions - preferably in your industry. This is not the time to call the lawyer who helped you write your will, or your cousin who does personal injury work. You need someone who knows the legal and regulatory complexities of business sales and has navigated them successfully before.

Your M&A Attorney's Role is to:

- Review and draft contracts
- Identify legal risks
- Advise you on deal structure
- Protect your interests through documentation and negotiation support

However - and this is crucial - your attorney should NOT negotiate your deal for you. Marty puts this plainly: attorneys are notoriously bad negotiators. That's not their strength, and turning the negotiation over to them could kill your deal. Your attorney's job is to make you aware of legal risks so you can make informed decisions, not to try to eliminate every possible risk and, in doing so, scare away the buyer.

The Tax Advisor: Protecting Your Net Proceeds

Selling your business comes with tax consequences—some obvious, others hidden. A qualified tax advisor with experience in business transactions can help you minimize your tax liability while staying fully compliant with the law.

Your Tax Advisor's Responsibilities Include:

- Reviewing deal structures to understand tax implications and minimize your tax burden
- Advising on how to time and allocate payments (e.g., asset sale, stock sale, goodwill allocation, etc)
- Coordinating with your M&A Attorney and Acquisitions Advisor to ensure consistency

Marty advises having an initial conversation with your tax advisor regarding your comfort level with risk. A good advisor will ask, "On a scale from nearly audit-proof to orange jumpsuit, where do you want to land?" Jokes aside, this underscores the importance of aligning your tax strategy with your values and your risk tolerance. You want to pay only what you owe in taxes, no more and no less.

The Acquisitions Advisor or Broker: Your Strategic Guide

Whether you choose to work with a business broker or a more hands-on acquisitions advisor, this member of your Exit Team is your quarterback. Their mission is to bring qualified buyers to the table, negotiate on your behalf, and structure a deal that reflects the true value of your business.

A Skilled Advisor Will:

- Prepare your business for market
- Attract and vet prospective buyers
- Coordinate due diligence
- Structure the transaction in a way that works for you & the buyer

They also play a critical coordination role between your attorney and tax advisor, ensuring the deal is both legally sound and financially optimized. And, when possible, they'll work to create a competitive bidding environment to drive your price up.

Bonus Members: Don't Overlook These Critical Voices

Beyond your professional advisors, there are two additional "team members" whose involvement can make or break your experience: your spouse/life partner, and your business partners (if any).

Your Spouse or Life Partner

Even if they don't work in the business, your spouse will be deeply affected by the sale. What happens after the check clears? Retirement? A new venture? Travel? Golf? A condo in Cabo? Selling your business is not just a financial decision—it's a life decision. Make sure your partner is on board and part of the planning process.

Your Business Partners

If you have minority investors or co-owners, they need to be fully informed and aligned with your exit strategy. Don't let an obscure clause in a years-old partnership agreement derail your deal at the eleventh hour. Marty recalls a transaction that nearly fell apart when a fractional partner's right-of-first-refusal clause was discovered deep in due diligence. Don't let that be your story.

When and How to Assemble Your Exit Team

The answer to "when" is simple: at least three years before you plan to sell. That runway gives you time to prepare, clean up your financial statements, and work with your advisors to make your business as attractive - and valuable - as possible.

As for "how," start with personal referrals. Talk to other business owners who have sold recently. Ask who they used, what went well, and what they would do differently. Referrals from one member of your Exit Team to others are also valuable, they'll already know how to work together.

Above all, look for advisors who listen to your goals, explain your options clearly, and are committed to helping you achieve the outcome you want.

The Bottom Line

Don't risk compromising your life's work by going into the sale process alone or with the wrong advisors. Assemble an Exit Team that's experienced, aligned, and committed to your success. Because when the time comes to walk away, you want to do so with confidence, peace of mind, and as much money in your pocket as possible.

Section I: FAQs

The Top 10 Questions Owners Ask About Selling Their Business

Businesses Valuations are Based on Fundamentals, Not Potential

As you will learn below, the number one question owners have about selling their business is, "What is my business worth?" And, if you're like most business owners, you have a number in mind which you believe - or at least hope - your business will sell for. Unfortunately, nine times out of ten, the number you have in mind is much higher than what the marketplace is willing to pay.

Marty once received a phone call from the widow of a recently-deceased owner of a plumbing business. Although he had died very suddenly, his widow remembered him once telling her that the business would be worth about three times its annual sales. So, when she called Marty, she thought he could help her fetch $1.5 million for the business, since it had generated $500,000 in sales during its last full year in business.

Sadly, because the plumbing company only consisted of her late husband running service calls in an ancient work truck, the value of the business after his death was almost zero. The difference between what she and her husband had THOUGHT the business would sell for, vs its actual value in the marketplace, came down to one thing - lack of knowledge. They didn't understand what the sale price of a business is based upon. Giving you that knowledge is one of the foundational missions of this book and all of our other educational resources.

But, what if your business was actually worth many times what you placed its value at? Could such a thing actually happen? And how could you not know that you were sitting on a gold mine? Again, the answer comes down to lack of knowledge.

One day, a seller called Marty about a business he'd been trying to sell through a local business broker. The listing had been live for months with no serious offers. The seller was frustrated, but not surprised. After all, he was asking what he felt was a "reasonable" price but, like many owners, he figured he'd be lucky to get that much.

Just like the plumber and his wife in the previous story, he didn't understand what buyers place value on when considering the purchase of a business. Only this time, he had aimed too low. Almost unwittingly, he had built a business that was lean, highly profitable, and poised to scale rapidly. Within a few hours of reviewing the company's financial statements, Marty called the owner back and said, "You're not asking too much, you're asking way too little."

They pulled the listing, revamped the pitch, and doubled the asking price. Then they targeted strategic buyers instead of more commonplace business buyers. The final deal not only delivered more cash up front than the previous listing's entire sale price, it also included equity in a larger firm, dramatically increasing the seller's long-term upside. Marty estimates that the value of that seller's stake today is somewhere between eight and twelve times what he was originally willing to sell the business for.

The moral of both of these stories is: Understand your current valuation and then get to work increasing that number.

"Potential" Belongs to the Buyer

One last thought before we get into the Top 10 Most Frequently Asked Questions: never try to sell - or even place a value on - the "potential" you believe your business has going forward. Any potential the business may have in the future will belong to the buyer and is theirs to exploit. Both Frank and Marty have heard this boast about "potential" many times from owners. Marty's standard response is, "If the potential is so great, why haven't you done it?" Frank's pat reply is, "If there's so much potential here, why don't you stick around and realize it?"

If your business really does have a lot of unrealized potential, the best favor you can do yourself is to spend the next three years tapping into it while moving your company to sale-ready condition. Create a growing book of business, maximize profits, implement a business operating system - take all the other steps we recommend. The book you are reading right now gives you every resource you need to make those things happen, resulting in the highest sale price possible in a deal with the optimal buyer, one who will take the best care of your employees and your legacy after you leave.

FAQ #1
How Much Is
My Business Worth?

If you're like most business owners, the first question that comes to mind when considering a sale is, "How much is my business worth?" And that's completely understandable—after all, the value of your business represents the payoff for years, maybe decades, of hard work, sacrifice, and dedication. But here are three honest truths:

- There is no simple answer

- Today, your business is probably worth much less than you think it is or wish it could be

- It's possible to dramatically increase its value over the next three years - or next 12 months, if you're in a hurry.

Why Valuing a Business Isn't Simple

Most of us are familiar with how tangible assets are valued. If you want to sell your car, you can look it up on Kelley Blue Book. If you're selling a house, you can check Zillow or ask an appraiser to pull market comparables and give you a clear idea of its worth based on square footage, number of bedrooms, and recent sales.

Unlike a car or a house, you can't just plug your business information into an online tool and get an accurate valuation. A business is more complex - it's a living, breathing entity, and its value depends on a wide range of factors.

A business valuation can vary widely based on:

- **Industry Trends** – Is your industry growing or shrinking?

- **Performance Trends** – Is your business growing, plateauing, or declining?

- **Location** – Is your market area thriving or struggling?

- **Operational Autonomy** – Is your business systematized and capable of running without you?

All these variables affect the value of your business. A potential buyer will also consider how much risk they're taking on and how much return they can expect based on your business's profitability and future potential.

Different Valuations for Different Purposes

There are different ways to calculate the value of your business, depending on the purpose of the valuation. Here are some of the most common methods:

- **Revenue-Based Valuation** – Often expressed as a multiple of annual revenue. This is simple but can be misleading, as revenue alone doesn't account for expenses or profitability. Also, this measure is most often used in high-growth industries such as technology or software and does not apply to most small businesses.

- **EBITDA** (Earnings Before Interest, Taxes, Depreciation, and Amortization) – This valuation focuses on your business's core profitability and excludes non-operating expenses and is often used with more "traditional" businesses.

- **SDE** (Seller's Discretionary Earnings) – Used for small businesses, SDE includes the owner's salary, perks, and any discretionary expenses that wouldn't necessarily continue under new ownership.

Each method will yield different numbers, which can create confusion. For example, accountants often focus solely on the numbers found in financial statements and may arrive at a higher theoretical valuation. But a business broker or acquisition advisor might give you a lower, more market-based valuation that reflects what buyers are actually willing to pay.

It's similar to getting a diamond appraised for insurance purposes. The appraisal may state that your diamond is worth $100,000. But if you were to try to sell it, would you actually get $100,000? Probably not. The market value—what someone is willing to pay—may be significantly lower.

Understanding Multiples in Business Valuation

No matter which valuation method is used - whether it's EBITDA, SDE, or another approach - the final number is typically expressed as a multiple of those earnings. In simplest terms, this multiple is the number by which your business's annual profit is multiplied to estimate its market value. However, the size of that multiple can vary widely depending on several key factors.

One of the most significant factors influencing your multiple is the industry you're in. For example, businesses in high-demand sectors like technology, healthcare, and recurring home services often command higher multiples due to their growth potential and buyer interest. In contrast, industries facing stagnation or heavy competition may see lower multiples. Another important factor is whether or not your business has predictable revenue streams, such as a subscription model or long-term contracts. Buyers place a premium on consistent, recurring cash flow, as it lowers their risk and provides a more stable return on investment.

Maximizing The Value of a Car Wash Business

A great example of how recurring revenue or a subscription model can impact the value of a business can be found in the seemingly humble car wash industry. Marty often explains how a car wash with multiple locations doing $12 million in annual top-line revenue and throwing off around $2 million in profit would normally sell for about $6 million, or a multiple of three times profit. But if that car wash derived most of its revenue from drivers who subscribe to their "Clean Car Club," providing a predictable stream of income every month, that same business could sell for as much as $14 million to $18 million.

That figure represents a multiple of seven to nine times profit. How could that be if, in terms of day-to-day operations, both companies are identical? Answer: the second business will sell for millions more due to its ability to generate predictable recurring revenue.

Other factors impacting your multiple include your "customer concentration" (is your revenue highly dependent on one or two large customers?), scalability (can the business expand easily with minimal capital investment?), and the degree of owner dependency (does the business rely heavily on your involvement in order to function?). Each of these variables can raise or lower your multiple, which is why the same dollar amount of profit can yield vastly different valuations in different scenarios.

The Impact of Company Size on Multiples

The size of your business also plays a significant role in determining its earnings multiple. Generally, larger companies - those with higher annual revenues - command higher multiples at sale compared to smaller businesses. This is because larger companies are often perceived as more stable, resilient, and capable of generating consistent cash flow, making them more attractive to potential buyers.

They also may have stronger brand recognition, larger customer bases, more diversified revenue streams, and well-established operational processes that reduce perceived risk for the buyer. As a result, a business generating $10 million in annual revenue may receive a multiple of 6 to 8 times its earnings, while a business generating $1 million annually may only receive a multiple of 3 to 4 times.

Buyers, especially private equity firms and strategic acquirers, often use company size as a proxy for operational maturity and market strength. They know that larger companies can typically scale more effectively and absorb market shocks more easily. Additionally, larger companies may have key performance metrics, such as profit margins and EBITDA, that make them ideal acquisition targets, which creates competition among buyers and drives multiples even higher.

Considering Equity in a Larger Organization

When considering selling your business to a private equity firm or a roll-up organization, you may be offered the opportunity to accept part of your payment in stock rather than cash. While this can feel uncertain at first, it's important to consider the potential upside.

By becoming part of a much larger, diversified organization, your stake in the combined company could eventually be worth a significantly higher multiple than your current business. For example, if your standalone business would sell at a 2-3x multiple of earnings today, but the larger organization plans to exit at an 8x multiple after further acquisitions and scaling, your future payout could be many times more than what you would have received by selling for all cash today.

Private equity firms and roll-up organizations often aim to create "economies of scale" by combining multiple smaller businesses into a single, more powerful entity. These larger entities typically enjoy enhanced negotiating power, reduced operational costs, and increased market share, which can drive their valuation far beyond the sum of the individual businesses. By taking some of your proceeds in stock, you align your financial success with the future growth of the combined organization, giving yourself the opportunity to benefit from that higher eventual valuation.

For example, when selling a sporting goods company to a private equity-backed rollup in his twenties, Marty and his co-founders took their $1.5 million payout entirely in cash and counted themselves as entrepreneurial geniuses. However, if they had chosen to take it all in stock instead, several years later their stake in the succeeding company would have been worth almost $24 million.

In spite of Marty's experience in this one case, and the story cited earlier in this chapter, this strategy isn't without risks. The future success of the acquiring entity depends on sound management and continued market performance. It's crucial to carefully evaluate the acquiring organization's track record, leadership, and growth strategy before agreeing to accept stock as part of your payout. Consulting with your Exit Team can help you determine whether taking an equity stake aligns with your personal financial goals and risk tolerance.

In short, the multiple reflects not just your business's current financial performance, but also its future potential and perceived risks. Understanding what factors increase your multiple can help you strategically position your business for a higher valuation and, ultimately, sell it for the highest possible price to the optimal buyer.

The True Definition of Value

Ultimately, your business is worth what a buyer is willing to pay and what you are willing to accept. That intersection, the meeting point of buyer and seller expectations, is the true value of your business. And it can be both enlightening and humbling.

Buyers don't see your business the same way you do. While you see years of hard work, sacrifice, and your reputation in the community, buyers see numbers, risk, and (hopefully) opportunity. That's why preparation and positioning are so important - they allow you to highlight your business's strengths and minimize any perceived weaknesses.

FAQ #2
When Is the Right Time to Sell My Business?

As business owners, we've all heard the familiar adage "buy low, sell high." But when it comes to selling your business, it's surprisingly easy to fall into the trap of doing the opposite, selling when things are tough rather than when everything's running smoothly. The best time to sell your business is when it's performing at its peak, not when it's stagnating or declining.

That said, timing isn't just about business performance. There are three more key factors to consider when determining the right time to sell:

- **Your Personal Timing:** Is this the right time for you and your family? Are you considering retirement, managing a significant life event, or simply ready for a new chapter? Personal readiness often plays the biggest role in choosing when to step away.

- **Your Business's Life Cycle:** Where is your business in its growth curve? If it's steadily growing or at its peak, you're in an ideal position to get top dollar. If it's plateauing or in decline, you risk selling at a lower valuation.

- **Market Conditions:** What's happening in your industry and the broader market? Are buyers active and willing to pay premiums, or is the market sluggish? Selling during an industry upswing or when financing options are strong can boost your sale price significantly.

Start Preparing 3–5 Years in Advance

One thing we say with confidence is that today is not the right day to sell. Ideally, you should begin preparing your business for sale at least three years before your target exit date. This gives you time to strengthen your financial statements, create efficient systems, and optimize your business so that it's attractive to the right buyers. The more time you spend preparing, the smoother and more profitable the transaction will be.

In the Boomer Sells the Business Workbook, we walk you through the steps you need to take to position your business for the highest possible price and identify the optimal buyer. By following this guidance well in advance, you'll avoid last-minute scrambling and ensure you're ready when the right time comes.

FAQ #3
How Do I Prepare
My Business for Sale?

When it comes to preparing your business for sale, you may be tempted to ask for a "quick checklist." But the reality is that getting your business sale-ready involves a series of detailed steps, and there's no shortcut to doing it right.

That's why we created the Boomer Sells the Business Workbook - to walk you through every step in an actionable, straightforward way. If you have a copy of the workbook at hand, turn to Section II: Seven Steps to Sale Ready Condition to guide you through successfully completing the steps synopsized below, and explained in greater detail later in this book.

These are our Seven Steps to Sale-Ready Condition:

1. Get Your Financial Statements in Order
Buyers want to see clean, accurate, and complete financial records. Your financials should provide a clear picture of your business's profitability and cash flow, with no "red flags" or confusing discrepancies. Having an experienced bookkeeper or accountant review and organize your statements can make a world of difference.

2. Implement an Operating System
A formal business operating system ensures that your processes and workflows are documented and repeatable. Think of this as the "instruction manual" for your business. It helps the next owner step in and run things smoothly without relying on you for day-to-day decisions.

3. Create an Owner Exit Plan

A business that is too dependent on you, the owner, is less valuable. Your exit plan should include training key team members and empowering them to take on your responsibilities so that the business can thrive even in your absence.

4. Identify Your Buyer Type

There are different types of buyers, from individual entrepreneurs to private equity firms or competitors. Understanding who your likely buyer is and tailoring your preparation to appeal to them is a strategic move that can significantly impact your sale price.

5. Set Your Valuation Target

As discussed in the first FAQ, understanding what your business is worth and setting a realistic valuation target is key. This not only helps you stay grounded in your expectations but also identifies the improvements you need to make to meet your goals.

6. Maximize Profit

Increasing your profit margins before a sale can substantially raise your valuation. This could mean streamlining operations, cutting unnecessary expenses, or boosting revenue with strategic marketing. Buyers are drawn to businesses that show steady, sustainable profit growth. This is also the time to talk to your tax planner about moving from a "tax mitigation" strategy to a "profit maximization" strategy.

7. Start Preparing Now

Ideally, you should begin preparing three to five years before your intended sale date. But even if you're planning to sell sooner, the most important takeaway is to start NOW. If you wait until you "have" to sell, you'll miss the opportunity to optimize your business and may leave money on the table.

FAQ #4
Who Will Buy My Business?

If your business is doing well and you've made the decision to sell, one of the most important questions you'll face is: Who is the right buyer? Understanding the different types of buyers helps you not only prepare your business for sale, but also to tailor your messaging to attract the optimal buyer - someone willing to pay the highest possible price and ensure your business thrives under new ownership.

The Boomer Sells The Business Workbook offers worksheets to help you identify potential buyers, assess their suitability, and plan your approach. In this section we break down the most common buyer types. The list of potential buyers outlined below is also covered in greater detail in Section III: Chapter 4, Identify A Buyer Type.

Common Types of Buyers

Family Members
A family transition is a common path, especially for owners who have built a multi-generational legacy. However, it's important to ensure that your chosen family member is prepared and motivated to take the reins. Ask yourself: Do they truly want this role, or are they feeling obligated? Family dynamics can complicate what should be a business decision, so clear communication and formal agreements are essential.

Key Employees

Your most dedicated team members know your business inside and out, making them ideal buyers. An internal sale often provides continuity for your customers and employees, which can be a priority for many owners. If you're considering this path, it's important to develop leadership within your team and explore financing options that make it feasible for employees to buy in, such as installment payments or profit-sharing agreements. Look for more information about selling your business to your employees through an ESOP (Employee Stock Ownership Plan) or MBO (Management Buyout) in Section V: Financing.

Competitors

While selling to a competitor may seem counterintuitive, it can be a creative strategic move. Competitors may see acquiring your business as a fast way to expand their market share, enter new geographic regions, or gain access to your customer base. The potential downside is that you'll need to be cautious about sharing sensitive information too early in the process. A non-disclosure agreement (NDA) is essential when engaging with competitors, and we highly recommend you bring in an independent third party (such as an Acquisitions Advisor and/or Attorney) to facilitate the conversation and protect you from sharing "too much too soon" with a direct competitor.

Vendors and Customers

Suppliers, distributors, and even loyal customers may see an acquisition as a way to strengthen their business. A key vendor may benefit from vertically integrating your operations into theirs, while a customer might acquire your business to ensure continued access to your products or services.

Third-Party Buyers

This category includes individual entrepreneurs, private equity firms, and investor groups looking for a profitable business they can either run directly or manage as a hands-off investment. Third-party buyers typically look for businesses with strong cash flow, clear operating procedures, and minimal reliance on the current owner.

Identifying the Right Buyer for Your Business

Every buyer has different priorities, and your choice of buyer should align with your goals for the sale. Consider the following questions:

- Do you want to exit quickly, or are you open to a longer transition period?

- Is preserving your company culture and taking care of your employees a top priority?

- Is your main objective to sell for the highest possible price, regardless of who the buyer is?

The answers to these questions will help you focus on the buyer type that best fits your situation.

For example, if you're aiming for a quick exit and the highest possible price, a third-party buyer may be the best fit. However, if your top priority is preserving the business legacy and taking care of your employees, a sale to key employees or a family member may be the better option, even if it means a longer transition or a slightly lower offer.

Molding Your Business to Match Your Optimal Buyer's Desires

Once you've identified the preferred buyer type for your business, the next step is to prepare your business and your marketing message to prospective buyers accordingly. For example, if your preferred buyer type is a third party entrepreneur, investor, or private equity group, now is the time to start working toward meeting the financial targets those buyers focus on.

Using the Workbook to Clarify Your Buyer Strategy & Messaging

The Boomer Sells The Business Workbook includes helpful guidance for identifying potential buyers, evaluating their strengths and risks, and preparing for discussions. In particular, Section IV: Identify a Buyer Type and Mold Your Business to Suit Them, can help you:

- Assess your personal priorities for the sale.

- Consider all possible buyer types and weigh their pros and cons.

- Prepare key information that buyers will want to see, such as financial summaries and operational plans.

FAQ #5

What Are the Tax Implications of Selling My Business?

When selling your business, taxes are an unavoidable factor, and their financial impact can be significant. However, neither of the authors of this book are licensed tax professionals, and it would be improper for us to provide tax advice. Instead, we strongly recommend that you consult with a licensed tax expert who specializes in business acquisitions to receive guidance tailored to your specific situation.

While we cannot provide tax advice or guidance, we do want to outline some general tax-related factors that sellers should be aware of as they plan their exit strategy. Knowing these factors will help you have informed discussions with your Professional Exit Team.

Key Tax Implications to Consider

1. Capital Gains Taxes
One of the most significant taxes associated with selling a business is the capital gains tax. This tax applies to the profit you earn from selling your business assets or stock. Long-term capital gains (on assets held for over a year) are typically taxed at a lower rate than short-term gains. Your financial advisor can help determine the portion of your sale subject to these rates.

2. Ordinary Income Taxes
In some cases, parts of your sale may be taxed as ordinary income rather than capital gains. This can happen when payments for consulting agreements, earnouts, or other forms of compensation are included in the sale structure.

3. Allocation of Purchase Price

When you sell a business, the purchase price is often allocated across different asset categories, such as equipment, goodwill, and inventory. This allocation can affect how much of your sale is taxed at capital gains rates versus ordinary income rates. It's critical to work with your tax advisor to optimize this allocation.

4. State and Local Taxes

Depending on where your business operates, you may be subject to additional state and local taxes. Some states have no capital gains taxes, while others have significant tax burdens. Understanding your state's tax obligations is an essential part of planning.

5. Self-Employment Taxes

If part of your sale involves ongoing compensation (such as through a consulting agreement or an earnout), that compensation may be subject to self-employment taxes, which can add to your overall tax liability.

6. Tax Implications of Installment Sales

In some cases, business sales are structured as installment sales (seller financing), where the buyer makes payments over time. This may spread out your capital gains liability across multiple years, but it may also have specific tax rules and potential risks to consider.

7. Potential Deductions and Tax Credits

There may be opportunities for deductions or credits, such as legal and professional fees associated with the sale. However, these deductions vary based on the type of business and the sale structure, so professional guidance is essential.

8. Entity Type Considerations

The tax implications of your sale may vary based on whether your business is structured as an LLC, S-Corp, C-Corp, or partnership. Different entity types have different tax treatments during a sale, and this can significantly impact your final net proceeds.

FAQ #6
What Documentation
Do I Need to Sell My Business?

When preparing to sell your business, one of the most critical steps is gathering the necessary documentation to give buyers a clear and comprehensive view of your financial health, operational performance, and growth potential. While the process can be tedious, the fact is that having your documents in order not only speeds up the sale of your business but also helps you negotiate for the highest possible price from the optimal buyer.

In this section, we'll walk you through the key documents you'll need to compile, referencing Step I: Get Your Financial Statements In Order found in the Seven Steps to Sale-Ready Condition section of The Boomer Sells The Business Workbook. Required Documentation will also be covered in more detail in Section III: Chapter 1, Get Your Financial Statements in Order of this book.

Here are the documents prospective buyers will want to see:

1. Profit and Loss Statements
A profit and loss (P&L) statement summarizes your revenue, costs, and expenses over a specific period—usually monthly, quarterly, or annually. This document demonstrates your business's profitability and shows how well your business has managed its operations. For buyers, the P&L is a fundamental resource to understand your bottom line and evaluate any trends that could impact the future performance of the business.

2. Balance Sheet

A balance sheet offers a snapshot of your business's financial standing by listing its assets, liabilities, and owner's equity at a specific point in time. Buyers use the balance sheet to assess the financial stability of your business and ensure that the value of your assets exceeds your liabilities. It's a crucial tool for demonstrating solvency and long-term viability.

3. Cash Flow Statements

Cash flow statements track the movement of money in and out of your business and provide valuable insights into your ability to cover expenses, repay debts, and fund growth. Unlike the P&L, which focuses on profits generated irrespective of cash received, cash flow statements reveal whether your operations generate enough cash to sustain and grow the business. Buyers want to see consistent, positive cash flow to confirm the financial health of your business.

4. Tax Returns (Last Three Years)

Your business tax returns are an official record of your reported revenue and taxable income. Buyers often compare your tax returns with your financial statements to verify accuracy and consistency. Having at least three years of tax returns available helps establish credibility and gives buyers a clearer picture of how your business has performed over time.

5. Accounts Receivable Report

This report lists all outstanding invoices and payments due from your customers, along with due dates and amounts. Buyers use this report to assess the reliability of your customer base, evaluate collection timelines, and gauge the potential risk of unpaid debts. A well-maintained accounts receivable report reassures buyers that your cash flow won't be disrupted by slow or delinquent payments.

6. Accounts Payable Report

An accounts payable report outlines what your business owes to vendors and suppliers, including due dates and outstanding balances. This report helps buyers understand your short-term financial obligations and avoid unexpected liabilities. Buyers want to know that your financial commitments are manageable and that they won't be burdened by unpaid debts or overdue invoices.

7. Detailed List of Business Assets

A comprehensive list of your business assets should include both tangible assets (such as equipment, inventory, and vehicles) and intangible assets (such as trademarks, patents, or customer databases). Buyers need this list to understand what physical and intellectual resources they will acquire as part of the sale. Providing a clear valuation of these assets can help you justify your asking price.

8. Depreciation Schedules

Depreciation schedules show how your assets have decreased in value over time due to use or age. Buyers use these schedules to determine the current book value of your assets and identify items that may need repairs or replacement. Depreciation schedules also highlight tax-related benefits that the buyer may inherit, such as remaining depreciation deductions.

9. Loan Documentation

Loan documentation includes agreements for any outstanding debts, such as business loans, credit lines, or equipment financing. These documents should specify the repayment terms, interest rates, and remaining balances. Buyers want to understand your debt obligations and whether they will need to assume or renegotiate any loans as part of the transaction.

10. Sales Records

Sales records provide detailed insights into your revenue streams, customer base, and sales trends over time. These records can help buyers identify seasonal fluctuations, high-value customers, and growth opportunities. Reliable sales records demonstrate that your reported revenue is accurate and consistent.

11. Expense Records

Your expense records detail the costs of running your business, including payroll, rent, utilities, and supplies. Buyers analyze these records to understand your cost structure, spot potential inefficiencies, and assess profitability. Accurate and complete expense records allow buyers to evaluate how they can maintain or improve the business's profit margins.

12. Inventory Reports

If your business relies on inventory, you'll need to provide reports that document the quantity, type, and value of your stock. These reports help buyers evaluate inventory turnover rates, identify obsolete or slow-moving items, and assess whether the inventory valuation aligns with your financial statements.

13. Projected Financial Performance

Projections provide an estimate of your business's expected financial performance over the next one to three years. Buyers often request this information to understand your business's growth potential and set realistic expectations for future profitability. Projections should be based on historical performance and market trends to ensure they are credible and defensible.

Key Takeaway

Having the right documentation ready is essential for a successful sale. Not only does it instill confidence in buyers, but it also empowers you to negotiate from a position of strength. By assembling your financial and operational records, you'll be well prepared for every step of the sales process. And, by taking the time to prepare your documentation, you'll set yourself up for a smoother transaction and increase the likelihood of selling your business for the highest possible price to the optimal buyer.

FAQ #7
What is the Biggest Mistake Owners Make When Selling Their Business?

When it comes to selling your business, there are two critical mistakes that can dramatically impact the outcome of your sale. The first, and by far the most common, mistake is failing to adequately prepare. The second, almost as damaging, is waiting too long to sell, often trying to sell only when the business is struggling instead of when it's at its peak.

The Number One Biggest Mistake: Failing to Prepare

Preparation is the cornerstone of a successful business sale. Many business owners underestimate the time, effort, and strategy needed to successfully position their business for a profitable exit. Whether you're driven by retirement, a desire to pursue new ventures, or unforeseen circumstances, preparation ensures your business is attractive to potential buyers and achieves the highest possible price.

Adequate preparation typically starts at least three years before you plan to sell. This gives you time to optimize your financial records, implement efficient operating systems, strengthen your management team, and address any weaknesses that could lower the value of your business. However, preparation isn't just about planning for a sale on your terms—it's also about safeguarding your financial future in case you're forced into an unplanned sale.

Life is unpredictable, and events such as Divorce, Disease, Death, Debt, Disagreements, or Burnout (the Five Ds and a B which are addressed in detail later in this book) can force you to sell your business unexpectedly. Without preparation, a forced sale often results in a lower sale price - or no sale at all.

Imagine trying to sell your business at a fair price while dealing with a health crisis, partnership dispute, or financial hardship. In such situations, you may be forced to accept a subpar offer simply because you lack the time and energy to make your business market-ready. By contrast, if your business is always in sale-ready condition, you'll be better positioned to negotiate and secure the best possible outcome, regardless of the circumstances.

This book and its Companion Workbook are designed to help you avoid this mistake by guiding you through every step of the preparation process, ensuring you're not only ready for a planned sale but also protected from the financial and emotional fallout of an unplanned sale.

The Second Biggest Mistake: Waiting Too Long to Sell

In the world of investing, there's an old adage: "Buy low and sell high." While that advice is easy to understand in theory, many business owners do the opposite when it comes to their own companies. They ride the wave of success for as long as possible, believing that growth and prosperity will continue indefinitely. However, when the inevitable downturn arrives - whether due to market changes, personal burnout, or economic factors - they find themselves trying to sell when the business is already on a downward trajectory.

Selling when your business is struggling generally results in lower offers and fewer interested buyers. Potential buyers may view the decline as a sign of deeper issues, even if the downturn is temporary or market-driven. Conversely, selling when your business is performing well positions you to negotiate from a place of strength. Buyers are more likely to pay a premium for a business that is growing and profitable.

It's natural to hesitate when things are going well - you're enjoying the rewards of your hard work, and selling might feel premature. However, the best time to sell is when your business is thriving, not when you're facing declining revenues or personal fatigue.

FAQ #8
How Long Does It Take
to Sell My Business?

The length of time required to sell a business varies greatly. In some cases, it can happen within a matter of weeks; in others, it can take years. While there's no universal timeline, there are key factors that influence the process, many of which you can control by preparing in advance.

The Role of Preparation in Accelerating the Sale

One of the most important ways to shorten the timeline is to ensure your business is in sale-ready condition before you list it. Comprehensive preparation means getting your financial documents in order, implementing an effective operating system, and reducing the business's reliance on you as the owner.

When your business is well-prepared, buyers will have fewer questions, and the due diligence process will move faster. Preparation can also reduce the likelihood of deal delays caused by missing or unclear information, boosting buyer confidence and ensuring smoother negotiations.

As we emphasize throughout this book and in the workbook, advance preparation gives you a significant advantage. The earlier you begin, the more leverage you'll have, and the less stressful the process will be.

The Pitfalls of a Quick Sale

If you're forced to sell quickly - whether due to an emergency or poor planning - you'll likely encounter significant disadvantages, such as:

- **Lower Sale Price:** A quick sale usually means accepting a lower offer. Buyers know that time pressure weakens your negotiating position, and they may offer far below market value.

- **Limited Pool of Buyers:** The faster you need to sell, the fewer qualified buyers will be available, especially those willing to meet your price and terms.

- **Stress and Disruption:** A rushed sale compresses every step of the process. You'll need to juggle buyer meetings, document preparation, and negotiations, all while running your business. This added pressure can be overwhelming and negatively affect your business performance.

- **Suboptimal Buyer Selection:** Selling quickly may limit your ability to find the optimal buyer - someone who aligns with your goals, such as preserving your company's legacy or protecting your employees. A rushed sale increases the risk of selling to the wrong buyer, which can lead to regrets down the line.

Macro Factors Beyond Your Control

Some factors that affect the timeline are external and beyond your control, such as changes in interest rates, capital availability, or economic downturns. These macroeconomic variables can either lengthen or shorten the sales process depending on market conditions. For example, when the Small Business Administration (SBA) recently adjusted its down payment rules, it opened up financing options that significantly increased buyer interest for some businesses.

However, you can mitigate the impact of market fluctuations by ensuring your business is well-positioned to attract buyers in any economic climate. The more attractive your business is operationally and financially, the better your chances of closing a sale, even when market conditions are challenging.

Key Takeaway

While you can't predict the exact timeline for selling your business, you can influence it by preparing thoroughly and starting early. Adequate preparation helps you avoid the disadvantages of a rushed sale and maximizes your chances of finding the optimal buyer at the highest possible price.

If you already own the Boomer Sells The Business Workbook, turn to Section II: Seven Steps to Sale-Ready Condition and refer to Step I: Get Your Financial Statements In Order, and Step III: Create an Owner Exit Plan to ensure your business is sale-ready. By investing time in preparation now, you'll be better equipped for a smooth and successful sale later.

FAQ #9
How Much Will It Cost
to Sell My Business?

When selling your business, you'll need to account for professional fees, document preparation, commissions, and other transaction costs. Even if you choose to sell the business yourself, you can expect to pay around 4-5% for legal and accounting fees. If instead you choose to hire a business broker or acquisitions advisor to do most of the heavy lifting for you, you can anticipate paying another 10% or so of the sale price in commissions.

So, generally speaking, you should budget between 5% and 15% for the cost of successfully selling your business. Keep in mind, however, that with the right team and preparation, these expenses are an investment that will likely increase your net proceeds rather than diminish them.

Factors Affecting Costs

The total cost can vary depending on:

- **Type of Buyer:** Selling internally to a family member or key employee may incur lower costs compared to marketing your business broadly to third-party buyers or private equity firms.

- **Scope of Services:** The level of assistance you require from your deal team can impact fees. Full-service advisory support will generally cost more, but can also lead to a higher sale price.

How The Right Team Can Maximize Your Net Proceeds

While the percentage fees may seem significant, it's essential to consider the value that a skilled team adds to the process. With the right professionals in place, you are more likely to:

- **Sell for a Higher Price:** Advisors can help identify ways to increase your business's valuation and negotiate with buyers to secure a better offer.

- **Minimize Tax Burden:** A tax expert can structure the sale to optimize capital gains treatment and avoid unnecessary penalties or liabilities.

- **Avoid Costly Mistakes:** Your legal team ensures that all agreements protect your interests, avoiding expensive litigation or disputes down the line.

By contrast, trying to manage the process alone can lead to costly errors, missed opportunities, and a potentially lower sale price.

Preparation Reduces Transaction Costs

Proper preparation before listing your business can further mitigate transaction costs:

- Organizing your financial records and having clear operating procedures in place can speed up the due diligence process, reducing legal fees and negotiation time.

- A well-prepared business is more attractive to buyers, which can reduce marketing expenses and shorten the sale timeline.

FAQ #10
What Will Happen to My Employees After I Sell My Business?

For many business owners, the most emotional aspect of selling their business is the potential impact it will have on their employees. After years—sometimes decades—of working side-by-side, your team can often feel like an extended family. In some cases, they literally are family members. It's only natural to wonder what will happen to them after the sale. The reality is, what happens to your employees largely depends on who buys your business and how you structure the deal.

The Impact of Buyer Type on Employee Retention

Different types of buyers have different goals, and those goals will influence how they treat your employees post-sale:

- **Private Equity Firms and Investment Groups:** These buyers often integrate your business into a larger portfolio. If they already have established back-office functions like accounting and HR, your current employees in those roles may face redundancy. This doesn't necessarily mean the entire team will be replaced, but you may have less control over who stays and who goes.

- **Entrepreneurial Buyers:** Individual entrepreneurs are more likely to maintain the status quo, especially if your business is running smoothly and profitably. These buyers often want to keep key employees to ensure continuity, as they are focused on preserving what made your business successful in the first place.

- **Strategic Buyers:** Competitors or vendors buying your business to expand their market share or secure supply may take different approaches. Some may retain your team to strengthen their operations, while others may streamline processes, resulting in some roles being eliminated.

Protecting Your Team with Employment Agreements

One way to protect your employees is by including employment agreements as part of the sale. These agreements can require the buyer to retain key team members for a specified period, typically one to two years. However, it's important to remember that adding too many stipulations regarding employee retention may deter some buyers, particularly private equity firms or buyers looking to streamline operations.

Other times, certain lenders, such as SBA loan providers, may require assurances of continuity in leadership to minimize business disruption. Again, these requirements may only apply to high-level or "Key" employees, and may not apply to front-line or administrative positions.

Offering Sale Bonuses to Employees

Some business owners choose to offer sale bonuses to their employees, especially if there's a chance they may lose their jobs after the sale. These bonuses serve as a form of severance, helping employees transition to new opportunities. While this isn't a requirement, it can be a meaningful way to show appreciation for your team's contributions to your successful sale while helping them land on their feet.

The Non-Poach Clause

A common clause in sale agreements is the "non-poach" clause, which prevents you from rehiring your former employees for a competing business or a new venture after the sale. These clauses typically last two to five years and are designed to protect the buyer from losing key talent immediately after the acquisition. Be sure to look for this in any purchase agreement you are given to review to ensure you are comfortable with the proposed terms.

Balancing Business and Personal Priorities

While it's admirable to want to secure your team's future, your top priority must remain achieving the highest possible price from the optimal buyer. In some cases, that buyer will value your team and retain them. In other cases, they may have different plans. The key is to know your priorities and communicate them clearly to potential buyers. By working with your legal team and acquisition advisor, you can strike a balance between saving your employees' jobs and making your business attractive to buyers.

Section II

Six Reasons Why You Should ALWAYS Have Your Business In Sale-Ready Condition

Why You Should Always Have Your Business Ready to Sell

When thinking about selling their businesses, most owners picture a future where they call the shots—planning their exit on their own terms, maximizing their payday, and stepping confidently into whatever comes next. Unfortunately, that's not how it plays out for most people.

In fact, according to figures published by the Business Enterprise Institute, the International Business Brokers Association, and the U.S. Chamber of Commerce, between 70 and 85 percent of business exits are triggered by unforeseen, uncontrollable events - what we call the 5 Ds and a B: Divorce, Disease, Death, Debt, Disagreement, and Burnout. And when one of those events hits, it doesn't come with a heads-up or a checklist. It arrives fast and can quickly become all consuming.

One story that brings this home involves a family-run business started by a young woman who had made a name for herself as an Olympic snowboarder and ESPN commentator. She launched a line of eco-friendly drinkware, with the idea of building it into an asset that could eventually be sold to fund her parents' retirement. She was the public face and marketer; while her parents handled operations and fulfillment. Things were going great. In just three years, they were bringing in several million dollars in annual revenue.

Then came the first diagnosis: one of her parents was told they had cancer. Within weeks, the second parent was also diagnosed. In an instant, a business that had been growing rapidly lost two-thirds of its leadership.

The focus of their energies shifted, and rightly so, to battling for their lives. And, due to that shift in focus, the business began to spiral. Sales dropped. Operations lagged. By the time they reached out to Marty for help selling, the business had been in decline for over a year.

Fortunately, Marty was able to find a buyer - someone compassionate, who understood the situation and still saw value in the brand. But the final sale price was a fraction of what it could have been if they had brought the business to sale-ready condition ahead of time. No systems were documented. No plan was in place for an unexpected transition. And the result was a loss of both equity and opportunity, at a time when the family could least afford it.

Stories like this are painful, but not uncommon. And we share them not to scare you, but to wake you up.

So if you're thinking, "I don't plan to sell for years," or "I'm not ready yet," just know this: The best time to get your business in sale-ready condition is always the same - right now. Because it's not just about positioning your business for a strategic exit on your terms. It's about protecting yourself, your family, your employees, and your legacy in case life throws you a curve ball.

In the pages that follow, we'll walk you through the six core reasons why your business should always be prepared for sale. Each of them is backed by real-life scenarios, owner experiences, and practical actions you can take starting today.

D1: Divorce

A Common but Often Overlooked Trigger for Selling Your Business

Divorce is one of the most disruptive personal events a business owner can experience, and it can often force the sale of a business - whether or not you are financially or emotionally prepared for it. While some business owners assume that their personal life and their business are separate, the reality is that a divorce can have significant legal, financial, and operational consequences that directly impact not only the daily operation, but also the value and saleability of your company.

If you're like many successful entrepreneurs, your business is your most valuable asset. In a divorce, that asset is often subject to division, just like a home, retirement accounts, or other marital property. Depending on how your business is structured and whether it was founded before or after the marriage, your spouse may be entitled to a portion of its value. In cases where the business is considered marital property, you may be required to buy out your spouse's share, which can create a financial strain so significant that selling the business becomes the only viable option.

Even if the business itself is not directly divided in the settlement, the financial demands of divorce - legal fees, alimony, and child support - can place an enormous burden on you as a business owner, potentially leading to a rushed or unplanned sale. A forced sale, especially under financial duress, often results in a lower valuation and fewer negotiating options. Instead of commanding the highest possible price from the optimal buyer, you may be forced to take the first reasonable offer that provides immediate liquidity.

The Emotional and Operational Toll of Divorce on a Business

Beyond the financial considerations, divorce can take a heavy emotional and operational toll that can impact your ability to manage your business. Running a company requires focus, energy, and clear decision-making. The emotional strain of divorce - stress, court proceedings, family conflicts - often leads to distraction, poor leadership, and an overall decline in business performance.

When an owner is mentally checked out, employees, customers, and partners notice. If productivity, morale, and customer satisfaction begin to suffer, the business's revenue and profitability may decline, which in turn reduces its market value.

Additionally, if both spouses were involved in running the business together, the separation can cause disruptions in leadership, daily operations, and even customer relationships. Long-term clients and employees may feel uncertain about the business's stability and future direction, leading to lost revenue and weakened team cohesion. If a divorcing couple cannot amicably agree on the future of the business, legal battles over ownership or control can delay decision-making and create instability that scares away potential buyers.

How to Protect Your Business from the Consequences of Divorce

The best way to protect your business from the devastating impact of divorce is to always keep it in sale-ready condition. This means running the company as though it could be sold at any time for the highest possible price. Whether or not a sale becomes necessary, taking steps to prepare ensures that the business remains strong, stable, and valuable in the face of personal upheaval.

Some Proactive Steps To Shield Your Business From Divorce-Related Risks Include:

- **Prenuptial or Postnuptial Agreements:** Whether you are considering marriage or are already married, a legal agreement can specify that your business remains separate property, preventing it from being divided in the event of divorce.

- **Buy-Sell Agreements:** If you have business partners, a buy-sell agreement can outline what happens if an owner gets divorced, preventing a spouse from gaining control of business shares.

- **Clearly Defined Ownership Structures:** Keeping clear legal records of ownership, including whether your spouse has ever played a role in the company, can help clarify what is subject to division.

- **Regular Business Valuations:** Periodic valuations help establish an accurate, up-to-date picture of your business's worth, which is useful if a buyout or sale ever becomes necessary.

- **Maintaining Clean Financial Records:** Well-organized financial statements ensure that if a division of assets or sale becomes necessary, you have clear documentation to support a fair valuation.

D2: Disease

How a Health Crisis Can
Force the Sale of Your Business

Serious illness or injury from an automobile accident are not uncommon reasons business owners are forced to sell their companies. Whether it's a sudden diagnosis, a long-term degenerative condition, or an unexpected medical emergency, disease can take you out of action faster than almost any other factor. If your business is not already in sale-ready condition, illness can force a rushed, poorly planned sale that results in a lower valuation and fewer options for a successful transition.

While many entrepreneurs focus on financial risks like market downturns and competition, you may underestimate the personal risks that could derail their business. When a health crisis strikes, your energy, focus, and ability to manage daily operations are suddenly compromised. Without a plan in place, your company—and its value—can begin to decline rapidly, making it difficult to sell on favorable terms.

The Double Impact: Personal and Business Strain

A serious illness affects more than just the business owner - it impacts employees, customers, vendors, and even family members who may be asked to step in and keep things running.

And when you become unable to lead the business, the effects are often immediate:

- **Operational Disruptions:** Without clear leadership, employees may struggle to make decisions, leading to delays, confusion, and inefficiency.

- **Revenue Decline:** Clients may hesitate to sign new contracts or continue business with a company facing leadership uncertainty.

- **Team Morale Issues:** Employees may be concerned about job security, leading to turnover at a time when stability is most needed.

- **Buyer Hesitation:** Potential buyers prefer to purchase businesses that are thriving, not ones in crisis. A business that appears unstable due to an owner's illness may scare off serious buyers or lead to reduced offers.

Forced Sales and Undervalued Exits

When illness forces an unplanned sale, you and your family can be placed at a significant disadvantage. A rushed sale typically results in:

- **Lower Valuations:** Buyers recognize urgency and will often negotiate aggressively, knowing the seller is under pressure.

- **Limited Buyer Pool:** The best buyers may not be available on short notice, forcing the sale to less-than-ideal candidates.

- **Weakened Financials:** A drop in revenue and profitability caused by the owner's absence can significantly reduce the company's worth.

- **Legal and Tax Complexities:** Selling a business under duress may lead to tax inefficiencies and poor deal structuring.

How to Protect Your Business from the Consequences of Disease

The best way to mitigate the risks of illness forcing a sale is to always keep your business in sale-ready condition. This means running your business in a way that allows it to function smoothly without your daily involvement. As discussed throughout this book and the companion workbook, key steps to achieve this include:

- **Creating a Business Operating System (BOS):** Establish clear processes and procedures so the company can run without you at the center of every decision.

- **Documenting a Leadership Succession Plan:** Identify a second-in-command or leadership team that can take over in the event of a medical emergency.

- **Training Employees for Key Roles:** Ensure that no single person, including yourself, is indispensable to daily operations.

- **Establishing a Power of Attorney:** Grant a trusted individual legal authority to make business decisions if you are unable to do so.

- **Building a Financial Safety Net:** Maintain healthy cash reserves and access to credit to sustain operations during unexpected disruptions.

Planning Ahead for a Stronger, More Valuable Business

Whether or not you plan to sell your business soon, preparing for the possibility of an unexpected health crisis is not just about protecting your own future—it's about ensuring the long-term survival and success of your company. Buyers prefer businesses that can operate independently of their owners, and a company that runs smoothly even during a health-related absence is far more attractive to potential acquirers.

D3: Death

The Unplanned Sale That No One Wants to Talk About

It's uncomfortable to think about, but the sudden or unexpected death of a business owner can force an immediate and often chaotic sale of their business. Unlike other factors in the Five Ds and a B, death is final and leaves no opportunity for you to participate in the transition. Without proper preparation, the burden of managing or selling the business falls entirely on surviving family members, partners, or employees - often with disastrous financial consequences.

A business that is not sale-ready when its owner unexpectedly passes away is highly vulnerable. Family members may lack the knowledge or expertise to run the business, employees may feel uncertain about their future, and customers or clients may take their business elsewhere due to instability. If the company's operations rely heavily on the owner, its value can plummet overnight.

The Consequences of an Unplanned Sale Due to Death

If you were to die unexpectedly and without the preparation we recommend, your company would face an instant crisis. Without a clear succession plan in place, the business may struggle to continue operating, and its value may decline rapidly.

The Most Common Issues In This Scenario Include:

- **Leadership Void:** Without a designated successor, key decisions may be delayed or mismanaged, leading to operational inefficiencies.

- **Financial Instability:** If you currently handle all financial matters personally, surviving family members may struggle to access bank accounts, settle debts, or maintain cash flow.

- **Legal Complications:** If ownership transfer plans are not clearly documented, disputes may arise among heirs, partners, or key employees.

- **Decreased Business Value:** Uncertainty about the company's future can scare away potential buyers or give them leverage to offer lower purchase prices.

- **Emotional Toll on Loved Ones:** The owner's death is already a painful event. Adding financial and business stress can make an already difficult time even worse for your family.

How to Protect Your Business and Your Family

Since death is unpredictable - but inevitable - preparation is the only way to safeguard your business, your employees, and your family's financial future.

This means ensuring that your business is structured in a way that allows it to continue operating, and be sold for full value, if something were to happen to you.

- **Have a Buy-Sell Agreement:** If you have business partners, a legally binding buy-sell agreement should outline what happens to your ownership stake if you pass away. This can ensure a smooth transition of ownership and prevent disputes.

- **Establish a Leadership Succession Plan:** Identify and train a second-in-command who can take over leadership responsibilities if needed.

- **Document Critical Business Processes:** If you are the only one who knows how to run certain aspects of the business, that's a problem. A business operating system (BOS) ensures that all critical processes are documented and that employees can keep operations running smoothly without you.

- **Ensure Proper Estate Planning:** Work with an estate attorney to establish a will or trust that includes clear instructions for your business. This will prevent legal battles among heirs and ensure your wishes are carried out.

- **Have Life Insurance for Business Continuity:** A "key person" life insurance policy can provide liquidity to cover business expenses or fund a buyout in the event of your passing. This can prevent the need for a rushed or distressed sale.

Start Preparing Today

Many business owners mistakenly believe they have plenty of time to prepare for a sale. But unexpected events can change everything overnight. If your business isn't ready to operate or transition without you, your family and employees could pay the price.

Now is the time to take action. Use the checklists in the Boomer Sells The Business Workbook to begin documenting your critical processes, identifying potential successors, and ensuring that your business is prepared for any eventuality.

D4: Debt

How Financial Pressures
Can Force a Sale

Debt is a double-edged sword in business. When managed wisely, it fuels growth, expansion, and increased profitability. But when it spirals out of control - whether due to rising costs, unexpected downturns, or poor financial planning - it can become a ticking time bomb that can force an owner to sell under less-than-ideal circumstances.

Many business owners assume they will have time to pay down debt before they decide to sell. But financial pressures can mount quickly, leaving them with little choice but to sell their business to cover obligations. Worse, a distressed sale due to overwhelming debt often results in a significantly lower valuation, meaning that even after the sale, the owner may still be left with financial burdens.

How Debt Can Compromise Your Sale

While some level of debt is expected in any business offered for sale, excessive or mismanaged debt can severely impact the saleability and valuation of your company. Here's how:

- **Reduced Net Proceeds:** Any outstanding business loans, credit lines, or other liabilities must be settled before the seller receives their payout. High debt levels can significantly reduce the amount of money you take home from the sale.

- **Buyer Hesitation:** Potential buyers may see a business with substantial debt as a risky investment, fearing that financial instability could make success difficult even after they take over.

- **Strained Cash Flow:** If too much of the company's revenue is allocated to servicing debt, there's less working capital available for operations, making the business less attractive to buyers.

- **Urgency Leads to Lower Offers:** If a business owner is forced to sell quickly due to debt pressure, buyers will sense desperation and use it as leverage to negotiate a lower price.

- **Personal Liabilities:** In many cases, business owners have personally guaranteed business loans, meaning that even after selling the business, they may still be held accountable for remaining debts if the sale price doesn't fully cover them.

When Debt Forces a Sale: Common Scenarios

Debt problems don't always come from poor financial management. External factors and market shifts can create sudden financial stress that leaves business owners with no option but to sell.

Some of the most common scenarios include:

- **Economic Downturns:** A recession or market contraction can lead to declining revenue, making it difficult to keep up with loan payments.

- **Rising Interest Rates:** If a business relies on variable-rate financing, sudden increases in interest rates can make debt unmanageable.

- **Bad Lease Agreements:** Some businesses are locked into high-cost leases with escalating rents that outpace revenue growth. A lease can become an unsustainable burden, forcing the owner to sell before profitability disappears completely.

- **Declining Industry Trends:** Certain industries face technological disruption or market shifts that erode profitability, leaving owners struggling to stay afloat.

- **Over-Leveraged Growth:** Some business owners take on significant debt to expand operations, only to find that revenue growth doesn't keep up with rising costs, putting them in financial distress.

Strategies to Protect Your Business from Debt-Driven Sales

The best way to ensure debt doesn't force you into a premature sale is to proactively manage your company's financial health and always keep your business in sale-ready condition. Steps to consider include:

- **Regular Financial Audits:** Conduct frequent reviews of your company's debt obligations and overall financial health to ensure you remain in control of your liabilities.

- **Avoid Over-Leveraging:** While borrowing can be a strategic tool, taking on excessive debt to finance expansion or operations without a clear repayment strategy can be dangerous.

- **Negotiate Favorable Loan Terms:** If possible, secure financing with fixed rates, longer repayment terms, or flexible payment structures to provide financial stability.

- **Build a Cash Reserve:** Having a financial buffer can help sustain the business during tough times and reduce dependency on borrowed funds.

- **Consider Refinancing:** If debt levels become concerning, refinancing to lower interest rates or better terms may be a viable option to reduce financial strain.

- **Ensure Clean Financial Records:** If a sale becomes necessary, well-organized financial records will help buyers assess the debt obligations more transparently and lead to a smoother transaction.

Debt and the Timing of Your Sale

One of the worst mistakes a business owner can make is to wait until financial distress forces a sale. If debt has already created instability, buyers will sense urgency and drive a harder bargain. The best way to maximize your business's value is to plan ahead - ensuring financial stability, controlling debt levels, and keeping the business positioned as an attractive investment.

If you're carrying debt and still want to sell for the highest possible price, taking proactive steps now will improve your position. The Boomer Sells The Business Workbook includes detailed financial preparation checklists to help you:

- Review outstanding liabilities and determine their impact on valuation

- Organize financial records for maximum transparency

- Identify strategies to improve cash flow before putting your business on the market

By taking control of your financial situation now, you can ensure that when the time comes to sell, you're doing so from a position of strength, not desperation.

D5: Disagreements

When Conflict Forces
the Sale of Your Business

Business partnerships, like marriages, often begin with optimism and a shared vision. But over time, disagreements can emerge, sometimes escalating to the point where continuing to work together becomes impossible. Whether it's a dispute over growth strategies, financial decisions, or leadership roles, unresolved conflicts can lead to an impasse that forces the sale of the business, often under less-than-ideal circumstances.

How Disagreements Can Lead to a Forced Sale

Disputes among owners can arise for a variety of reasons, including:

- **Different Visions for the Future:** One partner may want to expand aggressively, while another prefers a conservative, steady-growth approach.

- **Unequal Workloads:** When one partner feels they are carrying more of the burden while splitting profits equally, resentment can build.

- **Financial Conflicts:** Disagreements over reinvesting profits, distributions, or personal spending habits can create long-term tension.

- **Leadership Struggles:** Conflicting management styles or competing leadership approaches can make decision-making difficult.

- **Personal Issues:** Family disputes, personality clashes, or changes in personal priorities (such as retirement) can lead to growing friction between business partners.

When these disputes escalate and become unresolvable, a sale may be the only viable solution. However, when a business is sold due to internal conflict, the sale process is often rushed, emotional, and contentious - leading to a lower valuation and less favorable terms.

The Impact of Partner Disputes on Business Value

A business being sold due to ownership disputes can face several challenges:

- **Buyers Sense Distress:** When buyers learn that a business is for sale due to internal conflict, they may assume instability and use it as leverage to negotiate a lower price.

- **Distracted Leadership:** When partners are embroiled in disputes, business performance often suffers, further reducing valuation.

- **Operational Uncertainty:** Employees, suppliers, and customers may become anxious about the company's future, leading to turnover and lost business.

- **Legal Battles and Delays:** If partners cannot agree on terms, the sale process may be delayed by legal disputes, making the situation even worse.

Strategies to Avoid a Forced Sale Due to Disagreements

To prevent internal conflicts from escalating to the point of a forced sale, business owners should take proactive steps to manage partnerships effectively:

- **Create a Clear Partnership Agreement:** A well-drafted operating agreement should outline ownership percentages, decision-making authority, dispute resolution procedures, and exit strategies.

- **Define Roles and Responsibilities:** Clearly outlining each partner's responsibilities can help prevent disputes over workload and leadership.

- **Plan for Buyouts in Advance:** Having a buy-sell agreement in place ensures that if one partner wants to exit, the remaining owners have a structured process to buy them out. You may also want to explore provisions for a third party buy-out, where the entire business is not sold, but rather just the portion owned by the partner who wishes to leave the business is sold to a new partner.

- **Establish Regular Communication:** Scheduled leadership meetings to discuss goals, performance, and concerns can help prevent disputes from festering.

- **Use Mediation Before Litigation:** If conflicts arise, professional mediation can help resolve disputes before they escalate to legal battles.

If a Sale Becomes Inevitable, Control the Process

Despite best efforts, some partnerships reach a point where the only viable option is to sell the business. If this happens, it's essential to approach the sale strategically rather than reactively. The goal should be to maximize value and ensure a smooth transition rather than rushing into a deal out of frustration or desperation.

The Boomer Sells The Business Workbook provides critical guidance on preparing for a sale under any circumstances - including those driven by internal disputes. If disagreements among owners are making a sale likely, the Workbook's checklists can help you:

- Organize key financial and operational documents to maintain business value.

- Clarify your personal and financial priorities for the sale.

- Position the business for an optimal sale rather than a distressed transaction.

Final Thought: While disagreements among business owners are common, letting them escalate to the point of a forced sale is not inevitable. The best protection is preparation; ensuring that your business is structured in a way that allows for smooth ownership transitions if and when they become necessary. If you anticipate potential conflicts, now is the time to put agreements in place that protect your business, your employees, and your financial future.

Burnout

When Exhaustion Leads to an Unplanned Sale

Burnout is one of the most underestimated reasons you might find yourself forced to sell. Unlike financial struggles or external crises, burnout creeps up gradually—until one day, you simply have nothing left to give. The passion that once fueled the business fades, decision-making slows, and motivation disappears. The danger is that by the time you fully recognize that you are burned out, the business itself has already begun to decline, significantly reducing its value and attractiveness to buyers.

One way to anticipate burnout before it happens is to be on the lookout for a loss of passion for your business. Even if you haven't reached the point where you dread going into work, if you're occasionally feeling like you'd rather stay home watching daytime television, be sure to take note of those feelings. Look yourself in the mirror and have an internal conversation about how you really feel about continuing to be the owner of this business, before your change of heart starts affecting your finances.

How Burnout Affects Business Value

The symptoms of burnout don't just impact you personally; they directly affect the health and valuation of your business:

- **Declining Revenue and Profitability:** A burned-out owner often loses the drive to seek out new business opportunities, expand marketing efforts, or innovate. This leads to stagnation or even decline in revenue.

- **Reduced Employee Morale:** Employees take cues from leadership. When an owner is disengaged, it creates uncertainty and low morale among the team, leading to decreased productivity and higher turnover.

- **Operational Neglect:** A business owner struggling with burnout may start cutting corners, neglecting financial reviews, delaying strategic decisions, or allowing inefficiencies to persist.

- **Weaker Market Position:** Competitors who remain energetic and engaged will seize opportunities that the burned-out owner ignores, potentially weakening the company's market position.

- **Rushed and Desperate Sale:** By the time you decide to sell due to burnout, your business may already be in decline, making it harder to secure a high-value exit. Buyers prefer businesses with strong leadership and growth potential, and burnout often signals the opposite.

Recognizing the Warning Signs of Burnout

Burnout doesn't happen overnight. There are often warning signs that business owners should watch for:

- Feeling mentally or physically exhausted every day, even when the workload hasn't changed.

- Losing interest in business growth, new ideas, or strategic planning.

- Procrastinating on important decisions, projects, or meetings.

- Noticing increased employee frustration or turnover.

- Experiencing a loss of motivation, even for tasks that were once enjoyable.

When these warning signs appear, you need to take action before burnout starts affecting your company's performance and saleability.

How to Avoid Selling Your Business Due to Burnout

Avoiding burnout, and the need for a forced sale, requires a proactive approach:

- **Delegate More Responsibilities:** A business that relies too heavily on its owner is not only exhausting to run but also difficult to sell. Implement systems and train employees to take on key tasks so the business can function independently.

- **Create a Business Operating System (BOS):** A structured BOS helps standardize operations and ensure efficiency, reducing the stress and decision-making burden on the owner.

- **Step Away Regularly:** Taking regular vacations and time away from the business can help you regain perspective and prevent long-term exhaustion.

- **Develop an Exit Strategy in Advance:** Having a clear exit plan allows you to transition out of ownership on your own terms rather than being forced to sell in desperation.

- **Consider Partial Ownership Transfer:** You might find relief in selling a portion of your business to a partner, investor, or key employee, allowing you to scale back your involvement while still sharing in the financial benefits.

If Burnout Has Already Set In, Sell Smart

If burnout has reached a critical point and selling is the only viable option, you should still take steps to maximize your business's value before listing it for sale:

- **Get Excited About Selling the Business:** Find motivation in moving on from your business and into your next adventure. Then use that energy to take the steps listed below.

- **Re-Engage with Business Performance Metrics:** Even if the goal is to exit, improving financial performance in the short term can increase the sale price.

- **Identify the Right Buyer Type:** A competitor, key employee, or third-party investor may see the most value in acquiring the business and keeping it running successfully.

- **Avoid a Fire Sale Mentality:** Selling a business quickly out of frustration or exhaustion often leads to poor deal structures and lower valuations. Instead, take time to prepare and position the business for a strong sale.

Final Thought: Selling from Strength, Not Exhaustion

Burnout is real, and it can be just as damaging to a business as any financial or operational crisis. The key is to recognize it early and take action before it forces a rushed, undervalued sale. Whether you ultimately decide to sell or find ways to reignite your passion, keeping the business in sale-ready condition ensures you always have options.

For practical tools to prepare for a sale or transition, you can use the Boomer Sells The Business Workbook to document processes, train employees, and create an exit strategy, ensuring that when the time comes to sell, you do so on your own terms, at the highest possible price, to the optimal buyer.

Section III

Seven Steps to Sale-Ready Condition

The Story of One Business Owner Who Did Everything Right

When we talk about getting your business into "sale-ready" condition, it can sound like an abstract concept. What does sale-ready really mean? What does it look like in the real world? Below is the real-life story of a business owner who did all the preparations we recommend, systematically, thoughtfully, and with remarkable success.

Kelly owned an interior design firm in a high-end suburb of Chicago. Now, if you're thinking, "Interior design? That's a business that lives or dies on the personal brand of the owner," you'd be right. Most such businesses are nearly impossible to sell because they're too dependent on the founder's taste, talent, and client relationships.

But Kelly's story was different - because Kelly chose to be different. She began preparing her business for sale five years before she intended to exit. She treated that goal like any other major project: with strategy, discipline, and a clear timeline. And in doing so, she became a living example of what we're teaching in this book.

Here's how Kelly aligned her actions with each of the Seven Steps to Sale-Ready Condition:

1. Financial Statements in Order

Kelly hired a dedicated financial advisor to prepare her business for sale. Her financial statements were pristine—down to the penny. Everything reconciled: profit and loss, balance sheets, tax returns, and bank statements. Due diligence? Already done.

2. Operating System Installed

Knowing she had to remove herself from the day-to-day operations, Kelly spent years building a team that could run the business without her. She hired multiple designers and promoted one to a senior role. She also brought on a business manager to oversee operations. By the final year before the sale, she was taking more vacation time than ever, and the business was growing faster than ever.

3. Exit Plan Created

Kelly didn't just plan to exit, she planned how, when, and to whom she wanted to sell. She knew what kind of buyer she wanted and why: someone who would preserve her legacy, respect her team, care for her clients, and grow the business. And, when the time was right, she brought her plan to Marty and his team.

4. Buyer Type Identified

She envisioned a younger, energetic and ambitious buyer who could take the reins and carry the company forward. The buyer she ultimately found was exactly that - someone who shared her values and had a vision for the future. Financing came via an SBA loan, so the business had to meet all the requirements of that rigorous process - and it did.

5. Target Valuation Modeled

Unlike many sellers, Kelly had a realistic understanding of what her business was worth. She worked with valuation professionals and didn't let emotion cloud her expectations. She focused on facts, not fantasies and increased the company's value over time.

6. Profit Maximized

Kelly stopped chasing revenue and started maximizing profit, because she understood that valuation is based on earnings, not top-line growth. She made strategic decisions to reduce unnecessary expenses and show maximum profitability on paper and in the bank.

Prepared Early

This is where Kelly really set herself apart. She didn't wait until she was burned out. She didn't wait until life forced her hand. She started the process five years in advance. That allowed her to move at a reasonable pace, make smart decisions, and ensure the business would be healthy and attractive when it was time to sell.

Since selling her business, Kelly is living a life she designed as carefully as the interiors her firm once created. She stays involved with her former firm on a limited basis - consulting when it's fun, not because she has to. She's stress-free, financially secure, and moving closer to family in Florida to enjoy the next chapter of her life.

Kelly's success didn't happen by accident. It was the result of thoughtful preparation, realistic expectations, and taking action years before her planned exit.

This section of the book covers the Seven Steps that Kelly followed, the same ones that we recommend to every owner looking to sell their business. Each step is explained in detail, with guidance to help you apply it to your own business. This area of preparation is also uniquely supported by our Companion Workbook. If you haven't already picked it up from Amazon, now would be a great time to do so.

Step 1

Get Your Financial Statements in Order

One of the most common reasons business sales fall apart, or result in lower-than-expected valuations, is poorly maintained financial records. As Marty puts it, "Too many entrepreneurs run their businesses by simply checking their bank balance at the end of the month to see if they have any money left, instead of maintaining structured, accurate financial records." This approach might work for day-to-day survival, but when it comes time to sell, it can cost you hundreds of thousands - or even millions - of dollars in lost value.

If you want to sell your business for the highest possible price to the optimal buyer, you must get your financial statements in order long before you put your business on the market.

Why Accurate Financials Matter

Buyers don't just purchase a business based on what it does today, they buy based on its financial past, present, and future potential. Without clear, well-documented financials, buyers can't trust what they're seeing, and trust is the foundation of any successful business transaction. If your records are incomplete, disorganized, or inconsistent, buyers may:

- Lower their offers to account for unknown financial risks.

- Walk away from the deal entirely due to a lack of confidence.

- Take longer to complete due diligence, delaying the sale.

Simply put, having clean, clear financial records makes your business more valuable and easier to sell.

Key Financial Documents You Need to Prepare

At a minimum, you need to have the following financial documents ready before putting your business on the market:

1. Profit & Loss Statements (P&Ls): Last 3-5 Years

Your P&L statements give buyers insight into how much revenue and profit your business generates each year. They should be accurate, consistently categorized, and up-to-date. Any unexplained fluctuations or missing data will raise red flags with buyers.

2. Balance Sheets: Last 3-5 Years

A balance sheet shows what your business owns (assets) and what it owes (liabilities). Buyers use this document to understand your company's financial health, debt levels, and net worth. If your balance sheet is messy or inconsistent, buyers may assume your finances are in worse shape than they actually are.

3. Tax Returns: Last 3-5 Years

Most buyers and lenders use tax returns to verify the accuracy of financial statements. If there's a big discrepancy between the income you reported on your tax returns and what's in your financials, expect questions. Be prepared to explain any anomalies.

4. Accounts Receivable and Accounts Payable Reports

Buyers will want to know:

- How much money is owed to your business? (Accounts Receivable)
- How much money does your business owe to vendors and creditors? (Accounts Payable)

A business with large, overdue receivables or unpaid vendor bills can be seen as a financial risk. Keeping these reports clean and current reassures buyers.

5. Cash Flow Statements

Your cash flow statement shows how money moves in and out of your business. Even a highly profitable business can fail if it doesn't have good cash flow. Buyers want to see steady, predictable cash flow, not wild swings that may indicate financial instability.

6. Capital Expenditures (CapEx) and Asset List

If your business has significant equipment, vehicles, real estate or other property, buyers need to understand:

- What assets your business owns
- How much they are worth
- How often major purchases or replacements are required

A well-documented CapEx plan reassures buyers that they won't be blindsided by major expenses after taking over.

7. Financial Projections (Next 3-5 Years)

Buyers don't just care about the past - they want to know where the business is headed. A clear financial projection shows:

- Expected revenue and profit growth
- Anticipated expenses
- Expansion plans or market opportunities
- Risks and contingencies

Even if projections aren't 100% certain, they help buyers see the business's potential and justify a higher purchase price.

Common Financial Reporting Mistakes That Can Hurt Your Sale

Even businesses with strong financials make mistakes when preparing for a sale. Here are the most common pitfalls to avoid:

- **Mixing Personal And Business Finances:** If you run personal expenses through the business, buyers may question the accuracy of your financials. (This is one of the most common issues we see)

- **Inconsistent Record Keeping:** If different years use different accounting methods, buyers may assume your numbers aren't reliable.

- **Not Reconciling Accounts:** If your financial statements don't match your tax returns, expect scrutiny.

- **Failing To Document One-Time Expenses:** If you've had large, one-time investments (e.g., a website rebuild, legal fees), be ready to explain them so they don't artificially lower your profitability.

- **Delaying Financial Cleanup:** Waiting until the last minute to organize your financials increases stress and can delay or derail the sale process.

How to Get Your Financials Sale-Ready

The good news is that even if your financials are a mess today, you can fix them before selling. Here's what you should do:

1. Hire a Professional
If you're not confident in your bookkeeping or accounting skills, hire a professional. A good CPA or financial consultant can help clean up your records and present them in the most favorable light.

2. Use Accounting Software
If you're still using spreadsheets or paper records, transition to a proper accounting system like QuickBooks, Xero, or NetSuite. These systems make it easier to generate reports and ensure accuracy.

3. Conduct an Internal Financial Audit

Before buyers start scrutinizing your numbers, do a deep dive yourself (or with your accountant). Look for:

- Inconsistencies or missing data
- Unexplained expenses or revenue fluctuations
- Areas where profits or costs need to be clarified

4. Improve Your Margins Before Selling

Since buyers will assess your business based on profit margins, now is the time to:

- Reduce unnecessary expenses
- Renegotiate supplier contracts
- Eliminate low-margin products or services

A healthier net profit margin will increase your business's valuation.

5. Use the Workbook to Organize Your Financials

The Boomer Sells The Business Workbook provides a step-by-step guide to getting your financial statements in order. In the workbook section aligned with this chapter, Section II: Seven Steps to Sale-Ready Condition, Step 1, you'll find:

- A financial checklist ensuring you have all key documents ready
- A list of red flags that could lower your business valuation

Guidance on working with accountants and financial advisors to optimize your sale

Final Thought: Buyers Love Financial Clarity

A business with clean, well-documented financial statements is far more attractive to buyers than one with disorganized or incomplete records. The better your financial records, the higher the purchase price you can command, and the more likely your business will sell quickly to the right buyer. If you need structured guidance, open your workbook and begin working through the financial preparation checklists today.

Step 2

Create a Business Operating System

Imagine your business as a well-oiled machine, where every cog moves seamlessly without needing your constant input. That's the power of a business operating system (BOS). At its core, a BOS is a structured framework that defines how your business runs - from day-to-day tasks to long-term strategy. It provides clarity, accountability, and consistency, ensuring that everyone on your team is working toward the same goals.

What Is a Business Operating System?

A business operating system is not a piece of software. Instead, it's a comprehensive methodology that organizes every function of your business. Think of it as a playbook that outlines what's expected of every team member, at every moment. It aligns your business's vision, communication, and processes, allowing your team to function as a cohesive unit, creating a much more attractive acquisition target for every buyer type.

Without a BOS, businesses often feel chaotic. Employees may have different priorities, communication breaks down, and the same problems keep resurfacing. By implementing a BOS, you establish a shared vision and a clear set of rules, enabling everyone to "row in the same direction." Proven systems like the Entrepreneurial Operating System® (EOS), Gazelles, and Scalable Operating System can serve as templates for building your own BOS.

Why Your Business Needs a BOS

Many business owners resist formalizing their business processes, fearing the time and effort it will take. But failing to create a BOS keeps your business reliant on you, making it difficult to scale and nearly impossible to sell. A BOS ensures your company can thrive without you at the center of every decision, creating a much easier business for a new owner to operate successfully.

When you implement a BOS, you achieve:

- **Increased Efficiency:** Documented processes reduce confusion and minimize wasted time and effort.

- **Improved Accountability:** Clear roles, responsibilities, and expectations help your team take ownership of their work.

- **Consistency:** Your customers receive the same high-quality experience, regardless of who's handling their service - or owns the business.

- **Saleability:** Potential buyers can see exactly how your business operates and will feel confident they can take over successfully.

The Franchise Playbook Analogy

Picture owning a franchise business such as a McDonald's. When you buy a franchise, you receive an operations manual that outlines every process, from unlocking the doors in the morning to hiring and firing, cooking the burgers, knowing exactly how many fries go in a "large" and, finally, steps for closing up at night. This manual is the franchise's BOS, and it ensures consistency across thousands of locations.

Your BOS should function the same way: as a comprehensive guide that allows someone else to step into your role and keep the business running smoothly. Marty often uses the analogy of a wagon wheel, where the owner is the hub and every operational process is a spoke connected to them. If you're the hub holding everything together, your business can't run without you. A BOS redistributes the weight so that the wheel can keep turning even if you're no longer at the center.

Key Elements of a Business Operating System

Vision and Goals: Your BOS should define your company's long-term vision and outline specific, measurable goals that keep your team aligned.

- **Processes and Procedures:** Document the key workflows for every department - from sales to customer service to finance - so your team knows exactly what to do and when.

- **Accountability Structure:** Assign clear roles and responsibilities, ensuring that everyone knows who's responsible for what.

- **Leadership Rhythms**: Establish regular team meetings to review progress, address challenges, and celebrate wins.

- **Performance Metrics:** Track key performance indicators (KPIs) in easy to understand "dashboards" to monitor progress and make data-driven decisions.

Preparing Your Business for a Smooth Handoff

A BOS doesn't just benefit you, it benefits your future buyer. Potential buyers want to know they can step into ownership without the business falling apart. By implementing a BOS, you provide them with a roadmap for continued success, making your business far more attractive and valuable. It also allows you to take a step back before the sale, demonstrating that your business can function independently - a critical factor for achieving the highest possible sale price.

Using the Workbook to Build Your BOS

In the Boomer Sells The Business Workbook, we walk you through the steps of documenting your processes, setting up your accountability structure, and establishing leadership rhythms. By following the checklists in Section III: Seven Steps to Sale-Ready Condition, Step 2: Create a Business Operating System, you'll learn nineteen important steps you should take across nine key categories:

- Vision and Strategy

- People and Roles

- Processes and Systems

- Meetings and Communication

- Data and Metrics

- Growth and Improvement

- Financial Management

- Customer and Market Focus

- Fostering a Positive Company Culture

Key Takeaway

Creating a business operating system may seem like a daunting task, but it's one of the most important investments you can make. A well-designed BOS not only makes your business more efficient and scalable—it also makes it more valuable and sellable. By putting the right systems in place, you're building a business that can thrive without you at the center, increasing its appeal to buyers and maximizing your exit strategy.

To learn more, watch or listen to the Boomer Sells The Business Podcast interview Frank and Marty did with Doug Wick, a strategic business consultant who specializes in helping businesses write and implement operating systems.

Step 3

Create an Owner Exit Plan

Exiting your business isn't just about selling it, it's about making yourself less essential to daily operations long before the sale happens. If your business can't run without you, then in the eyes of a buyer, you don't own a business - you own a job. That's a major problem when it comes time to sell.

Many business owners believe "exit" simply means selling and walking away. In reality, a successful transition involves multiple exit steps, each designed to make your company more independent, scalable, and attractive to buyers. The sooner you start stepping back, the higher your chances of selling for the highest possible price to the optimal buyer.

Why You Must Exit Before You Sell

There's an old saying in business: "The more valuable you are to your business, the less valuable your business is." This piece of wisdom was shared to Marty by one of his business mentors, Ryan Diess. In the years following, Marty has seen it proven true time and again. If your company revolves entirely around you - your knowledge, your decision-making, your customer relationships - then a buyer won't see it as a self-sustaining asset. Instead, they'll see risk.

Buyers want to acquire your business, not take over your full-time job. If you coming into work each day is the primary thing holding the business together, they'll either demand a lower price, require you to stay on for an extended transition period, or worse, walk away from the deal entirely.

Creating an Owner Exit Plan means reducing your business's dependence on you, improving its ability to thrive without your daily involvement, and increasing its attractiveness to buyers. This process happens in five key stages:

Exit Step #1: Step Out of the Day-to-Day Operations

The first phase of exiting your business is removing yourself from frontline tasks. If you're still the one "turning wrenches," processing transactions, or handling customer calls, your business is overly reliant on you and not yet sellable. The first step is making sure you're managing the business, not working in it.

To begin stepping back:

- Hire and train employees to take over key tasks.
- Develop standard operating procedures (SOPs) to document workflows.
- Establish clear performance expectations and accountability systems.

Exit Step #2: Step Out of the Staff Structure

Once you're no longer handling daily tasks, the next step is removing yourself from the organizational chart as an essential leader. If every decision still runs through you, then your absence will cause chaos for employees and uncertainty for buyers.

To achieve this:

- Appoint and train a General Manager or COO to oversee daily operations.
- Empower employees to make decisions without constantly checking with you.
- Implement a Business Operating System (BOS) so that processes are repeatable and scalable.
- Shift your role to strategic oversight rather than direct management.

At this stage, you're still the owner, but your company can function without your constant presence.

Exit Step #3: Step Out of the CEO Role

At this level, your business operates entirely without your involvement, but you remain as a board member or advisor.

Your key role shifts to:

- Offering high-level strategic guidance rather than managing operations.

- Attending quarterly or annual meetings instead of daily check-ins.

- Ensuring leadership succession is stable before selling.

By this stage, your business should be nearly indistinguishable from a franchise, where a new owner could step in and keep things running smoothly without you.

Exit Step #4: Fully Remove Yourself from Decision-Making

Some owners prefer to retain partial ownership in the form of dividends or profit-sharing without staying involved in daily operations.

This stage means:

- You no longer attend meetings, approve decisions, or oversee leadership.

- The business generates passive income, while the team runs everything.

This option is ideal for owners who want to step away but still collect financial returns.

Exit Step #5: Sell the Business and Walk Away

The final step is a full exit via sale, merger, or acquisition. If you've completed the previous steps, your business will be structured for maximum value, ensuring:

- Buyers see a turnkey operation, not a company that crumbles without you.

- Your team is prepared to support the new owner through the transition.

- You can negotiate favorable deal terms without being forced into an extended earnout period.

Many business owners fail to prepare for this step until it's too late, reducing their sale price and limiting their exit options. The earlier you begin implementing your exit plan, the stronger your negotiating position will be when the time comes to sell.

Overcoming Resistance to Exiting Your Business

Many owners struggle with stepping back. Even when they know it's necessary, they hesitate.

Sometimes, this hesitation comes from a love for the work—but more often, it's inertia. It's easier to keep doing what you've always done than to embrace change.

To overcome this resistance:

- **Accept That Stepping Back Increases Value:** Buyers want businesses that can run without the owner's involvement.

- **Redefine Your Role:** Instead of being the "boss," shift to being a mentor or strategic advisor.

- **Trust Your Team:** Train and empower them, then give them the space to operate.

- **Remember Your Long-Term Goal:** Whether you want to retire, start a new venture, or simply gain more freedom, making yourself non-essential is the key to achieving it.

Key Takeaway: Your Exit Starts Now

If you wait until it's time to sell to start your Owner Exit Plan, you'll already be too late. The sooner you step back from day-to-day operations, the more valuable your business becomes.

Use the Boomer Sells The Business Workbook to assess where you are in the exit process and develop a plan to reduce your company's dependence on you. By working through the checklists in Step 3: Create an Owner Exit Plan, you'll gain clarity on:

- Which stage of exit you're currently in.
- What steps you need to take next.
- How to transition smoothly while maximizing business value.

When the time comes to sell, you want to be exiting from a position of strength, not desperation. Start your Owner Exit Plan today to ensure you're in control of your future.

STEP 5

Identify a Buyer Type and Mold Your Business to Suit Them

When selling your business, you need to recognize that not all buyers are the same. Different types of buyers have different motivations, priorities, and expectations. By identifying who your most likely buyer is early on, you can shape your business into an ideal acquisition target, maximizing both its sale price and the likelihood of a smooth transaction.

Who Are Your Potential Buyers?

Before listing your business for sale, consider the different categories of buyers and what they look for in an acquisition. The following are some of the most common buyer types:

1. Entrepreneurial Buyer

An entrepreneurial buyer is often someone who wants to transition from employee to business owner or expand an existing small operation. These buyers are looking for businesses with stable revenue, solid operational systems, and an opportunity for hands-on growth.

What Entrepreneurial Buyers Want:

- A business that is operationally sound and well-documented
- An opportunity to increase revenue and profits quickly
- A smooth transition with available training from the seller

How to Attract Entrepreneurial Buyers:

- Ensure your financials are in excellent shape
- Create a Business Operating System (BOS) to facilitate a seamless handoff
- Offer training and support post-sale to ease the transition

2. Competitor or Industry Buyer
A direct competitor or industry buyer may acquire your business to expand their market share, eliminate competition, or gain access to your customer base and proprietary assets.

What Industry Buyers Want:

- A strong customer base and a recognizable brand
- Operational efficiencies and synergies to reduce costs
- A quick and seamless integration with their existing operations

How to Attract Industry Buyers:

- Strengthen your brand and customer loyalty
- Maintain clean, organized financial and operational records
- Identify ways your business can complement a competitor's existing operations

3. Vendor or Supplier Buyer
Suppliers, vendors, or even major customers may be interested in acquiring your business to control their supply chain, increase profitability, or enhance strategic partnerships.

What Vendor or Supplier Buyers Want:

- A way to vertically integrate their business for better cost control
- A reliable customer or supplier relationship they can benefit from long-term
- Operational stability and profitability

How to Attract Vendor or Supplier Buyers:

- Demonstrate how owning your business will improve their margins

- Maintain strong customer relationships to show value beyond raw financials

- Ensure your business can run efficiently with minimal owner oversight

4. Strategic Buyers

A strategic buyer is typically an entity looking to expand into a new geographic market, diversify their offerings, or leverage your business's resources in ways that complement their existing structure.

What Strategic Buyers Want:

- Unique assets such as intellectual property, customer contracts, or skilled employees

- A strong presence in the geographic or industry specific market they wish to enter

- Synergies that will allow them to scale quickly

How to Attract Strategic Buyers:

- Position your business as a valuable asset within your industry

- Develop transferable assets like brand equity, proprietary technology, or exclusive contracts

- Create a strong leadership team that can function without you

The Power of Rollups: A Special Buyer Type

One of the most active buyer categories in today's market is rollups, which are driven by private equity firms or larger corporations seeking to consolidate smaller businesses into a single, more powerful entity.

What Is a Rollup?

A rollup occurs when an investor or company acquires multiple smaller businesses within the same industry, and "rolls them up" under one corporate umbrella. This strategy provides economies of scale, brand consolidation, and operational efficiencies.

Examples of Rollups in Action

- **Waste Management Inc.:** Acquired over 130 small waste disposal businesses, becoming a national industry leader.

- **HVAC and Plumbing Industry:** Private equity firms are actively acquiring small home services contractors to create national brands.

- **Auto Repair Chains:** Many independent repair shops have been rolled into larger service networks for cost efficiency and market expansion.

Why Would a Business Owner Sell to a Rollup?

Selling to a rollup offers distinct advantages that many other buyers don't provide:

- **Higher Valuation Potential:** Rollups often pay higher multiples than individual buyers.

- **Economies of Scale:** Large-scale operations reduce costs and increase margins, making the business more profitable post-acquisition.

- **Faster Transactions:** Private equity-backed rollups usually have the cash to close deals quickly.

- **Retained Equity Opportunities:** Business owners may be able to sell a majority stake while keeping a percentage of ownership, benefiting from the future growth of the larger company.

Positioning Your Business for a Rollup Acquisition

If you want to attract a rollup buyer, you need to ensure your business meets their ideal criteria:

- **Scalability:** The business should be able to grow quickly and fit seamlessly into a larger operation.

- **Operational Independence:** A company that can function without heavy owner involvement is far more attractive.

- **Financial Transparency:** Rollups are financially driven, so clean, well-documented financial records are critical.

- **Subscription-Based or Recurring Revenue:** Businesses with predictable, recurring revenue streams often command higher valuations.

Key Takeaway

Understanding who your likely buyer is and aligning your business to meet their expectations is one of the most important steps in preparing for a sale. Whether you're targeting an individual entrepreneur, a strategic buyer, or positioning your business for a lucrative rollup, making your business sale-ready is the key to securing the highest possible price from the optimal buyer.

Use the Boomer Sells The Business Workbook to start identifying potential buyers, assessing their needs, and shaping your business to attract the most lucrative offers. With the right preparation, you can ensure your business is not only valuable today but positioned for an even greater exit in the future.

Step 5

Understand Your
Valuation Target

One of the biggest mistakes business owners make when selling their business is assuming it's worth far more than the market will actually pay. It's understandable - you've invested years, if not decades, building your company. To you, it represents countless hours of hard work, risk, and sacrifice. But the reality is that buyers don't see your business the way you do. They view it through the lens of financial performance, risk, and growth potential.

If you don't have a clear, data-backed valuation target, you could end up disappointed, frustrated, or forced to sell for far less than you expected. That's why getting an objective assessment of your business's value is a critical step in the sale-ready process.

Why Most Business Owners Overestimate
The Value of Their Business

Many business owners enter the sale process with an unrealistic number in mind. They assume that because their business has been "successful" it should command a high price. But valuation is determined by objective financial factors, not personal attachment.

One of the toughest conversations Marty has with sellers is explaining that their business is worth significantly less than they thought. A seller may believe their business is worth $2 million when, based on financials and market conditions, it's only worth $400,000..

This is why it's critical to determine what your business is worth NOW, as well as what it could be worth with strategic improvements. By taking the time to understand your valuation target early, you can make informed decisions and increase your business's sale price.

How Business Valuation Is Determined

Your business's value is typically based on a multiple of earnings. But what earnings means, and what multiple is applied, varies widely based on factors such as:

- **Your Industry:** Some industries command higher valuation multiples due to strong growth potential and stable recurring revenue.

- **Revenue and Profitability:** A business with strong, consistent profit margins is more attractive to buyers.

- **Business Size:** Larger businesses generally receive higher multiples because they are less risky.

- **Growth Potential:** Businesses with clear paths for expansion and scalability often attract higher offers.

- **Operational Independence:** A business that runs smoothly without the owner's daily involvement is far more valuable than one dependent on its owner.

- **Financial Cleanliness:** Well-documented, accurate financial statements increase buyer confidence and perceived value.

- **Market Trends and Timing:** Selling during a market upswing can mean a higher multiple, whereas selling during an economic downturn may lead to lower valuations.

How to Determine Your Business's Valuation Target

There are multiple ways to get a business valuation, and each has different costs and levels of accuracy. Here are the four most common.

1. Ask Your Accountant

Your accountant can provide a book value estimate, which calculates the value of your assets minus liabilities. However, this method doesn't consider market conditions, goodwill, or future earnings potential, so it's rarely a good indicator of actual sale value.

2. Ask a Business Broker

A reputable business broker can provide a market-based estimate based on comparable sales. If you choose this route, make sure to work with a broker who has experience selling businesses in your industry and geographic area. The wrong broker could overestimate or underestimate your business's worth.

3. Consult an Acquisitions Advisor

An Acquisitions Advisor goes beyond what a traditional broker offers. They not only help determine value but also provide strategies to maximize it. They specialize in creative deal structures, helping sellers achieve higher valuations through strategic positioning.

4. Hire a Certified Business Appraiser

A Certified Business Appraiser provides the most detailed and defensible valuation report. This is particularly useful if your sale involves legal considerations, such as a partner buyout or court proceedings. However, this option is the most expensive and may not always be necessary.

When to Get a Valuation

Many business owners wait until they're ready to sell to determine their business's value. This is a mistake. If you get a valuation early—three to five years before your planned sale—you give yourself time to make adjustments that could dramatically increase your sale price.

Consider this: If your business is currently worth $1 million, but you make strategic changes to improve financial performance, systematize operations, and enhance recurring revenue, in three to five years you may be able to increase its value to $2 million or more.

Maximizing Your Business's Value Before Selling

Understanding your valuation target isn't just about knowing what your business is worth today, it's about identifying what steps you can take to increase that number in the future. Here are key strategies to maximize value before putting your business on the market:

- **Increase Revenue and Profitability:** Buyers pay for earnings. Focus on growing revenue while improving profit margins.

- **Improve Financial Documentation:** Ensure your books are accurate, detailed, and easy for buyers to review.

- **Diversify Your Customer Base:** Businesses which are overly dependent on a single client are seen as risky. Spread revenue across multiple customers.

- **Reduce Owner Dependency:** If your business can't function without you, it's worth far less. Create systems and delegate responsibilities.

- **Lock in Recurring Revenue:** Subscription models, long-term contracts, and predictable cash flow increase buyer confidence.

- **Time Your Sale Strategically:** Selling during a strong economic cycle or industry upswing can lead to higher offers.

Key Takeaway

Your business's value is not set in stone, it is something you can influence and improve. The earlier you determine your valuation target, the more time you have to increase it.

If you want to sell for the highest possible price, don't wait until you're ready to exit. Get a valuation now, take steps to optimize your business's value, and ensure that when the time comes to sell, you're in the strongest possible position.

Use the Boomer Sells The Business Workbook to complete exercises that help clarify your business's current valuation and identify key areas for improvement. By taking action now, you can dramatically increase your final sale price and walk away with the financial reward you deserve.

Step 6

Maximizing Profit:
The Key to Increasing
Your Business Value

Maximizing your business's profitability before a sale is one of the most effective ways to increase its value and attract serious buyers. Profitability is not just about the money you take home, it is the primary factor that determines your business's valuation and the price buyers are willing to pay. Buyers want to acquire businesses that demonstrate strong, sustainable earnings, ensuring their investment generates a solid return.

A well-optimized, highly profitable business creates leverage during negotiations, giving you the ability to demand a higher sale price and attract the most desirable buyers. On the other hand, businesses with declining or unstable profits are viewed as high-risk, leading to lower valuations, longer sale timelines, and difficulty securing financing.

By implementing a series of strategic adjustments, you can boost your profitability and position your business for the highest possible sale price. The key areas to focus on include increasing revenue, reducing unnecessary costs, optimizing pricing strategies, improving cash flow, and ensuring your financials accurately reflect the true earnings of your business.

Profitability Drives Business Value

Business valuations are typically based on a multiple of your earnings, often measured by EBITDA (Earnings Before Interest, Taxes, Depreciation, and Amortization) or SDE (Seller's Discretionary Earnings), depending on the size and type of the business. The higher your profit, the higher the multiple you can command in a sale.

Another crucial factor is that most buyers use financing - such as SBA loans or commercial bank lending - to acquire businesses. Lenders will only approve financing for businesses with sufficient profit margins to cover both debt service and operational costs. If your business does not generate strong profits, buyers may struggle to obtain financing, reducing your pool of potential buyers and lowering your leverage in negotiations.

Beware of Tax Mitigation Strategies That Reduce Your Business's Value

It's common for business owners to minimize taxable income by using tactics such as writing off expenses, running personal costs through the business, or structuring finances to show lower profits. While these tax-saving strategies may reduce your annual tax bill, they can dramatically reduce your business's valuation when it comes time to sell.

Buyers rely on your reported profits to determine how much they are willing to pay. If your business shows little to no profit "on paper" it will appear unprofitable, even if you know it is generating strong cash flow. Since most buyers will assess the last three years of financial statements and tax returns before making an offer, you should plan ahead and ensure that your records accurately reflect the true earning potential of your business.

If you are currently operating with an aggressive tax mitigation strategy, you must decide what matters more - saving on taxes now or maximizing your business's sale price later. You cannot have it both ways. If you plan to sell in the next few years, begin adjusting your financial reporting today to show higher profitability.

And keep in mind, if your business is worth a 3x multiple of profits, for every dollar you save in taxes, you are giving up at least three dollars in valuation.

Practical Strategies to Maximize Your Profitability

1. Analyze and Improve Profit Margins

- **Evaluate Margins:** Identify which products or services have the highest and lowest profit margins.

- **Focus on High-Margin Offerings:** Shift your sales and marketing efforts toward the most profitable items.

- **Phase Out Low-Margin Products:** Consider discontinuing offerings that do not contribute significantly to your bottom line.

2. Reduce Operating Costs

- **Audit Business Expenses:** Review all expenses to identify areas where costs can be reduced.

- **Negotiate with Vendors:** Secure better terms and pricing from suppliers and service providers.

- **Automate Where Possible:** Implement automation in areas like customer service, billing, and scheduling to save on labor costs.

- **Outsource Non-Core Activities:** Sub-contract tasks that are not part of your core business operations to reduce overhead.

3. Optimize Your Pricing Strategy

- **Increase Prices Where Feasible:** Consumers are currently more accepting of price increases due to inflation. Test raising prices on high-demand products or services.

- **Introduce Tiered Pricing:** Offer premium options at higher price points to capture additional revenue.

- **Bundle Services or Products:** Creating package deals can increase the average transaction size and improve profitability.

4. Increase Sales Volume and Customer Retention

- **Upsell and Cross-Sell:** Train employees to recommend additional or complementary products and services.

- **Loyalty Programs:** Implement rewards programs to encourage repeat business.

- **Expand Market Reach:** Explore new customer segments, geographic areas, or online sales channels.

5. Enhance Revenue Streams

- **Introduce Recurring Revenue Models:** Subscription services, memberships, and retainers provide consistent, predictable cash flow, significantly increasing a business's value to buyers.

- **Diversify Offerings:** Expand into complementary products or services that align with your existing business.

- **Monetize Underutilized Assets:** Rent out unused office space, equipment, or intellectual property to generate additional revenue.

6. Improve Cash Flow and Accounts Receivable

- **Tighten Credit Policies:** Reduce the risk of late payments by requiring deposits or upfront payments from customers.

- **Strengthen Collections Efforts:** Actively follow up on overdue invoices to maintain strong cash flow and reduce Accounts Receivable.

- **Offer Discounts for Early Payments:** Encourage customers to pay faster with small discounts on early payments.

7. Streamline Operations and Reduce Waste

- **Conduct a Process Audit:** Identify inefficiencies and implement improvements to optimize workflows.

- **Minimize Waste:** Reduce material waste in production or service delivery to cut costs.

- **Invest in Employee Training:** A well-trained workforce operates more efficiently and makes fewer costly mistakes.

8. Reduce Debt and Interest Expenses

- **Refinance High-Interest Debt:** Secure lower interest rates to reduce monthly debt payments.

- **Prioritize Paying Off Debt:** Paying off loans before a sale can make the business more attractive to buyers and improve cash flow.

9. Regularly Monitor and Adjust

- **Use a Profit Dashboard:** Track key financial metrics weekly to ensure ongoing profitability.

- **Benchmark Against Industry Standards:** Compare your business's performance to competitors to identify areas for improvement.

- **Be Ready to Adapt:** Adjust strategies as needed based on market conditions and financial performance.

Key Takeaways

Buyers are willing to pay top dollar for businesses with strong profits, stable cash flow, and clear growth potential. By focusing on profitability now, you increase your valuation multiple, attract more buyers, and gain the upper hand in negotiations.

If you are serious about selling your business for the highest possible price, start maximizing profits today. A well-prepared, highly profitable business will command a stronger valuation and ensure that when the time comes to sell, you can do so on your terms.

Using the Workbook to Maximize Your Profitability

The Boomer Sells The Business Workbook contains practical checklists and financial assessment tools to help you:

- Identify profit-boosting opportunities.

- Track and optimize your most profitable revenue streams.

- Eliminate wasteful expenses and streamline operations.

- Implement pricing and sales strategies to increase revenue.

Step 7

Prepare Now

The best time to start preparing your business for sale was three years ago. The second-best time? Today. Preparing your business for sale is not an overnight task. It requires careful planning, strategic improvements, and financial optimization over time to position your business for the highest possible sale price to the optimal buyer.

If you've been following the steps outlined in this book, you already understand that a sale-ready business is a valuable business. Even if you don't plan to sell anytime soon, preparing now ensures you're never caught off guard by unexpected life events, market changes, or economic downturns.

The Power of Preparation: Why Start Today?

Many business owners assume they'll "get ready" to sell when the time comes. However, the reality is that the earlier you start, the more control you have over the outcome. Just to reiterate, here's why preparing now is crucial:

1. You Can Sell on Your Terms

When you prepare in advance, you dictate the timing, terms, and conditions of your sale. Business owners who wait until they have to sell often find themselves accepting less-than-ideal offers simply because they have no other choice.

2. Buyers Pay More for a Business That Runs Smoothly

Buyers aren't just looking for profitability, they want a business that can operate independently of its owner. If your company depends entirely on you as the owner, its value decreases dramatically. Preparing now allows you to build systems, train employees, and ensure your company can thrive without you, increasing its market appeal.

3. Market Conditions Change

Economic shifts, technological advances, and industry disruptions happen all the time. The more prepared you are, the better you can time your exit to maximize value. Selling a business when it's thriving, rather than when you're forced to, ensures you attract the best buyers and the best offers.

4. A Well-Prepared Business Is a More Profitable Business

The steps you take to get your business ready for sale - improving financials, streamlining operations, increasing efficiency - will likely make it more profitable for you while you still own it. In some cases, business owners find that after making these improvements, they no longer want to sell. Instead, they enjoy a more profitable, less stressful business that works for them.

The Risks of Failing to Prepare

Failure to prepare often leads to rushed sales, lower valuations, and unnecessary stress. If life forces you to sell unexpectedly - due to health issues, financial hardship, or market shifts - you could be forced to accept a significantly lower price than your business is truly worth.

1. Forced Sales Often Lead to Fire-Sale Prices

Marty has seen countless business owners who suddenly needed to sell their businesses "right away," only to realize they had done little to make the business attractive to buyers. Without proper preparation, even strong businesses can sell for pennies on the dollar - or worse, fail to sell at all.

2. Unexpected Life Events Can Derail Your Plans

As we discussed in Section II: Six Reasons Why You Should ALWAYS Have Your Business In Sale-Ready Condition, major life disruptions such as Divorce, Disease, Death, Debt, Disagreements, and Burnout can force a business sale at the worst possible time. If you haven't prepared in advance, these circumstances can leave you scrambling to find a buyer under unfavorable conditions.

3. Economic and Industry Disruptions Are Unpredictable

Throughout his career, Frank has personally experienced multiple business upheavals due to technological and economic shifts:

- His family's printing business was disrupted by the digital imaging revolution.

- An Internet business he co-founded was devastated by the dot-com bust.

- His residential real estate career collapsed in the 2008 financial crisis.

These kinds of disruptions can happen to any business, and those who aren't prepared are the ones who suffer most. The COVID-19 pandemic was a perfect example - entire industries were upended overnight. The businesses that survived (or even thrived) were the ones that had already built strong systems, financial stability, and contingency plans.

Practical Steps to Start Preparing Today

The best way to protect yourself from a forced or unfavorable sale is to treat your business as if you will sell it—even if you don't intend to in the near future. Here's how:

1. Know Your Valuation Now

Get a professional valuation so you understand where you stand today and what improvements you need to make to reach your target sale price.

2. Follow the Seven Steps to Sale-Ready Condition

Ensure you have clean financials, a business operating system, an owner exit plan, and a clear understanding of your ideal buyer.

3. Build Strong Leadership and Processes

Document key business processes, train employees, and make sure your company can run smoothly without you.

4. Eliminate Unnecessary Risk

Reduce debt, resolve legal or operational issues, and make your business as financially and operationally sound as possible.

5. Monitor Key Business Metrics

Track profitability, customer retention, and operational efficiency. Buyers want to see steady, predictable growth—not erratic performance.

Treat Sale-Readiness Like an Insurance Policy

None of us plan for a fire, but we have fire insurance. We don't plan to get into a car accident, but we have car insurance. Treat preparing your business for sale the same way - it's an insurance policy against the unexpected.

By getting your business in sale-ready condition now, you're giving yourself the best possible chance of selling for the highest price to the optimal buyer when the time is right for you. Whether you end up selling or keeping your business, the steps you take today will ensure you're in control of your future.

A Quick Request

To Help Another Business Owner Just Like You

Your Review Could Change a Life

You can get everything you want in life if you just help enough other people get what they want. — Zig Ziglar

If you've made it this far into the book, we know two things:

1. You're serious about preparing your business for a successful sale.

2. You're finding real value in the advice we're sharing.

Now we'd like to ask a simple favor in return.

There are millions of business owners out there, just like you, who are thinking about selling their business but don't know where to start.

Your review of this book could be the very reason they decide to pick up their own copy and begin the process of selling for the highest possible price to the optimal buyer.

We're on a mission to help as many of them as we can. But we can't reach them without your help.

Most readers decide whether or not to buy a book based on reviews. So, when you take a moment to leave yours, you're not just supporting us - you're giving another business owner the courage to move forward.

Your review could help...

- One more owner secure their retirement
- One more family preserve their legacy
- One more team keep their jobs and thrive
- One more community stay strong

It takes less than a minute and costs nothing, but it could mean everything to the next reader.

To leave your review, just scan the QR code below.

If you're the kind of person who believes in helping others take the next step, we want you to know that we appreciate your help more than words can say.

Thank you!

Marty & Frank

Section IV

The Sale Process:
15 Steps to The
Finish Line

The Sale Process

Selling your business is a complex, multi-step process that requires careful planning, strategic execution, and a team of skilled professionals. Whether you're selling to retire, pursue new opportunities, or respond to unforeseen circumstances, understanding each phase of the sale process will help you maximize your business's value and ensure a smooth transition.

This guide outlines the 15 essential steps to successfully selling your business, from making the initial decision to transitioning ownership to the buyer.

Step 1: Deciding to Sell

The decision to move forward with selling your business is not one to be taken lightly. You may choose to sell for personal reasons such as retirement, health issues, or burnout. Alternatively, financial factors like market timing, economic conditions, or a strategic acquisition opportunity might influence your decision. Regardless of the reason, take the time to evaluate your readiness and seek counsel from trusted advisors, including family members, financial professionals, and legal experts.

Step 2: Preparing The Business for Sale

Preparation is critical to securing the best possible sale price. A well-prepared business attracts more buyers and leads to smoother negotiations. Key preparation tasks include:

- Organizing financial records and ensuring clean bookkeeping.

- Implementing a Business Operating System (BOS) to reduce owner dependency.

- Optimizing profit margins and eliminating inefficiencies.

- Ensuring legal and tax compliance.

The more prepared your business is, the more appealing it will be to potential buyers.

Step 3: Selecting Your Exit Team

Surrounding yourself with the right professionals can make or break your sale. Your exit team should include:

- **Attorney:** Specializing in Mergers and Acquisitions within your industry.

- **Tax Professional:** Advises on tax implications and strategies to maximize your net proceeds.

- **Acquisitions Advisor (or Business Broker or Investment Banker):** Guides the sales process, finds buyers, and negotiates the best deal on your behalf.

Having this team in place before putting your business on the market ensures a well-executed transaction.

Step 4: Getting Your Business Valuated

Before listing your business, you need to determine its fair market value. A business valuation considers:

- Revenue and profitability.

- Industry trends and market conditions.

- Growth potential and competitive positioning.

Understanding your valuation helps set realistic expectations and allows you to negotiate from an informed position.

Step 5: Preparing Your Marketing Materials

Your business needs a compelling sales package to attract serious buyers. Your acquisitions advisor will prepare essential marketing materials, such as:

- **A Confidential Information Memorandum (CIM)** or **Prospectus** that outlines financials, operations, and growth potential.
- **A Buyer Profile** detailing the ideal buyer type and acquisition benefits.
- **A Teaser Document** that provides enough information to generate interest without revealing confidential details.

You play a key role in providing accurate and engaging details about your business.

Step 6: Putting Your Business on the Market

Once your materials are ready, your acquisitions advisor will launch the sale process. This may include:

- Listing on business sale marketplaces (e.g., BizBuySell).

- Leveraging industry networks and buyer lists.

- Conducting strategic outreach to potential acquirers, including competitors, vendors, and investors.

A well-marketed business attracts multiple buyers, leading to stronger offers.

Step 7: Vetting Your Buyers

Not every interested party is a serious buyer. Vetting buyers ensures that only financially qualified and strategically aligned individuals proceed in the process. This step involves:

- Assessing financial capability and funding sources.

- Evaluating industry experience and business compatibility.

- Having buyers sign Non-Disclosure Agreements (NDAs) to protect confidential business information.

A strong vetting process prevents wasted time and protects your business's sensitive data.

Step 8: Holding Buyer Discovery Meetings

At this stage, serious buyers meet with you and your advisor to learn more about the business. These meetings allow you to:

- Showcase your business's strengths and opportunities.

- Address buyer concerns and answer detailed questions.

- Gauge buyer intent and compatibility with your company culture.

Buyers may request multiple meetings as they conduct their own due diligence.

Step 9: Offer Negotiations

When buyers express interest, they submit an Offer Letter or Letter of Intent (LOI) detailing the proposed purchase price, terms, and conditions. You may receive multiple offers, requiring you to:

- Compare cash offers vs. seller-financed deals.

- Assess potential earnouts or stock options.

- Negotiate exclusivity clauses and due diligence timelines.

A skilled negotiator can structure the deal to maximize your financial outcome.

Step 10: Offer Acceptance

Once an offer is selected, you enter the exclusive or non-exclusive contract phase. Exclusive offers require you to remove your business from the market during due diligence, while non-exclusive offers allow continued negotiations with other buyers.

Terms such as earnest money deposits or breakup fees can be negotiated to protect both parties.

Step 11: Due Diligence

Due diligence allows the buyer to verify all financial, legal, and operational claims. Expect an exhaustive review of:

- Financial records (tax returns, bank statements, profit and loss reports).

- Employee contracts and vendor agreements.

- Business operations and key processes.

Having organized documentation in advance makes due diligence smoother and prevents delays.

Step 12: Purchase Agreements

Following due diligence, attorneys draft the final purchase agreement. This document finalizes:

- Purchase price and payment terms.

- Transition period obligations.

- Non-compete clauses and warranties.

Legal negotiations may take weeks before all parties agree on terms.

Step 13: Closing and Handoff

On closing day, the buyer funds the transaction, and ownership is legally transferred. Tasks include:

- Signing final agreements.

- Transferring business assets and accounts.

- Announcing the sale to employees and stakeholders.

With proper planning, this step ensures a seamless transition.

Step 14: Business Transition

Most sales agreements include a transition period (30-60 days) where you assist the buyer with:

Training key employees.

- Introducing new ownership to clients and vendors.

- Providing operational guidance.

If required, a longer consulting agreement may be negotiated.

Step 15: Post-Transition

After completing the transition, you officially move on to the next phase of your life. Some business owners remain engaged as board members or investors, while others step away entirely.

Whatever your next step, a well-executed sale ensures you exit on your terms and maximize your financial outcome.

Final Thoughts

Selling a business is a marathon, not a sprint. By following this structured approach and working with experienced professionals, you can navigate the complexities of the sale process confidently and profitably.

For additional resources and detailed checklists, refer to the Boomer Sells The Business Workbook, where we guide you step-by-step through preparing, negotiating, and finalizing the sale of your business.

Section V
Financing

Understanding How Buyers Will Fund the Purchase of Your Business

Many business owners picture their buyer arriving at the closing table with a briefcase full of cash. All you have to do is sign the papers and take the briefcase with you to Tahiti, where you will peel bills from it as needed to pay for your umbrella drinks.

In reality, very few small and mid-sized business transactions are funded with a single wire transfer, much less a briefcase full of cash. Most purchase offers involve a "stack" of financing sources - often a mix of bank loans, personal investment from the buyer, seller financing, performance-based earnouts, and so on. Each component of that stack carries a different level of risk and reward for you. And the overall structure of the deal impacts not only how much money you walk away with, but when and how you get it, and what happens if things go sideways.

That's why, even though you're not the one who has to secure financing, you need to understand the options available to buyers and what they will mean to you as the seller. Whether you're being asked to carry a note, agree to an earnout, or consider a management buyout, you need to understand how each financing method will impact your financial security.

In the chapters that follow, we'll break down the most common forms of buyer financing, show you how they typically work, and explain what they mean for you. By understanding the building blocks of acquisition financing, you'll be better equipped to evaluate offers, negotiate terms, and make sure you're getting the best possible outcome from the sale of your business.

SBA Acquisition Loans

For many buyers, securing financing is the single biggest challenge when acquiring a business. While cash offers and conventional financing options exist, one of the most widely used financing methods is an SBA Acquisition Loan under the SBA 7(a) program. This government-backed program provides a pathway for buyers who may not have enough liquid capital or collateral to purchase a business outright.

For you as the seller, understanding how SBA financing works - and its impact on your transaction - can help you prepare for a smoother sale and maximize your payout.

What Is an SBA Acquisition Loan?

The Small Business Administration (SBA) is a U.S. government agency that helps small businesses secure financing by guaranteeing loans issued by approved lenders. The SBA 7(a) loan program is specifically designed to support various business needs, including business acquisitions.

This program has grown increasingly popular in recent years due to its favorable terms for business buyers, including lower down payment requirements and longer repayment terms. Because of this, more buyers than ever are using SBA-backed loans to purchase businesses, potentially making your business more accessible to a wider pool of buyers.

Key Features of SBA 7(a) Loans for Business Acquisitions

- **Loan Limit:** The maximum loan amount under the SBA 7(a) program is $5 million. If the sale price of your business exceeds this amount, the buyer will need to secure additional financing sources to cover the difference. This can be done through seller financing, third-party loans, or private investment.

- **Down Payment Requirements:** Traditionally, SBA loans required a 10% down payment from the buyer which, in the past, could not be borrowed. However, recent changes now allow seller financing to cover part - or in some cases, all - of the down payment under certain conditions.

- **Repayment Terms:** SBA loans typically offer 10-year repayment periods with competitive interest rates, making them an attractive financing option for buyers.

- **Vetting and Approval Process:** Because the SBA guarantees a significant portion of the loan, the approval process is rigorous. Buyers must meet strict financial and credit qualifications, and the business itself must pass a detailed due diligence review before funding is approved.

- **Closing Timeline:** SBA loan approvals take time, typically 90 to 120 days from start to finish. While this timeline is slower than some other financing options, it provides a structured and reliable funding path for many buyers.

How SBA Loans Benefit You as the Seller

If your buyer is financing the acquisition through an SBA 7(a) loan, there are several important advantages for you as the seller:

1. Higher Likelihood of Full Cash Payment at Closing
Since SBA-backed loans provide structured funding, a business seller is more likely to receive 100% of the agreed-upon purchase price at closing (minus any seller-financed portion). Unlike other financing methods that involve deferred payments or earnouts, SBA deals typically allow sellers to walk away with a lump sum payment.

2. Buyer Prequalification and Vetting
SBA-backed buyers undergo a thorough vetting process by their lender, including personal credit checks, financial history reviews, and business experience assessments. This reduces the risk of dealing with unqualified or unreliable buyers.

3. Stronger Buyer Pool
Since SBA loans open business acquisitions to buyers who might not otherwise afford the purchase, more qualified buyers can compete for your business, potentially increasing demand and sale price.

The Downsides of SBA Loans for Sellers

While SBA financing is an attractive option for many buyers, there are some downsides for sellers:

1. Longer Closing Timelines
SBA loans take three to four months to finalize, which can be frustrating if you're looking for a quick sale. With an offer from a cash buyer or a buyer using private financing, the transaction may move much faster.

2. Intensive Due Diligence Requirements
The SBA conducts extensive financial and operational due diligence on your business to ensure it meets their lending criteria. This means you'll need to provide detailed financial statements, tax returns, profit and loss reports, and operational data, and you may be asked to provide additional documentation at multiple points in the process.

3. Potential Seller Financing Requirements

In some cases, you may be asked to finance part of the deal, especially if the buyer struggles to meet the down payment requirement. While this isn't mandatory, it's often encouraged to make deals more viable. If you do agree to seller financing, the SBA typically requires a "standby period" of two to three years, during which no payments on the seller-financed portion of the deal are made to you. However, interest will accrue during this period, meaning you could still profit from the arrangement in the long run.

SBA Rule Changes: Seller-Financed Down Payments

A recent rule change in the SBA 7(a) loan program allows sellers to finance part (or even all) of the buyer's required down payment in certain situations.

Traditional SBA Down Payment Rule

Previously, SBA required buyers to contribute at least 10% down, and that money had to come from personal savings, current investments, or other sources, it could not be borrowed.

Updated Rule: Seller Financing for the Down Payment

Now, under specific conditions, sellers can finance up to half of the buyer's required down payment. In rare cases (such as when selling to an internal employee or management team), the entire down payment may be seller-financed.

How This Affects Sellers

If you're asked to finance part of the down payment, you'll receive most of the sale price at closing, but a small portion will be repaid over time.

- You may not receive payments for the first two to four years, depending on the loan terms.

- The remaining balance will accrue interest (currently 8-9%) and will typically be repaid over a three- to five-year period.

- There is some risk of your loan not being repaid, but SBA approved buyers are heavily vetted, reducing the likelihood of default.

Is an SBA-Backed Buyer Right for You?

If your business meets the SBA's lending criteria and is valued at $5 million or less, an SBA-backed buyer may be an excellent option. However, you should weigh the pros and cons:

Best for Sellers Who Want:

- A large buyer pool and increased demand for their business

- A higher chance of full payment at closing

- Buyers who have been pre-vetted for financial stability

Less Ideal for Sellers Who:

- Need a quick closing (SBA deals take 3-4 months)

- Prefer a private sale with fewer documentation requirements

- Don't want to risk financing part of the down payment

Final Thoughts: SBA Loans as a Path to a Stronger Exit

For many business owners, an SBA-backed acquisition is the best path to securing a successful sale. While it requires patience due to longer closing times and in-depth due diligence, it often results in sellers receiving most (if not all) of their sale price upfront.

If your business is a strong candidate for SBA financing, working with an SBA-experienced broker or acquisitions advisor can help navigate the process, ensuring that both you and the buyer have a smooth transaction.

Before listing your business, consider discussing SBA loan eligibility with a qualified lender to understand how it may impact your sale. If a high percentage of your potential buyers rely on SBA funding, preparing for the documentation and timeline requirements in advance will help you avoid delays and increase the likelihood of a successful closing.

Next Steps

Use the Boomer Sells The Business Workbook to:

- Determine whether your business is a good candidate for SBA-backed financing

- Prepare the required financial documents in advance

- Understand the impact of seller-financed down payments on your payout

By doing this preparation upfront, you'll be in the best position to attract SBA-qualified buyers and close a profitable, hassle-free sale.

Conventional Bank Loans

For many buyers, an SBA loan is the most accessible path to financing a business acquisition. However, not all buyers qualify for an SBA loan, and in some cases, conventional bank loans provide a better alternative. While these loans do not come with the government-backed advantages of the SBA, they can still be a viable way for buyers to secure funding, especially for businesses that exceed the SBA 7(a) loan cap or do not meet SBA eligibility requirements.

Understanding how conventional bank loans work, their impact on the sale process, and what to expect as a seller is crucial to structuring a successful deal.

How Conventional Bank Loans Work

Conventional business acquisition loans are issued by commercial banks and other lending institutions without the guarantee of the U.S. government. This means that banks assume more risk, which affects how they structure the loan terms.

Some of the key characteristics of conventional bank loans include:

- **Higher Down Payment Requirements:** Unlike SBA loans, which typically require a 10% down payment from the buyer, conventional loans often require 20% or more.

- **Loan-to-Value (LTV) Ratios:** Conventional lenders will usually finance between 70% and 80% of the total business purchase price, meaning buyers must cover the remaining amount through a combination of personal funds, seller financing, or other investment sources.

- **More Flexible Loan Amounts:** SBA loans have a $5 million limit, but conventional banks may fund larger deals if the borrower has strong financial credentials and the business meets strong stability and cash flow criteria.

- **Shorter Closing Timelines:** Conventional loans can often close more quickly than SBA loans, usually taking 30 to 60 days, vs. SBA loans which typically take 90–120 days.

Because conventional loans require a larger down payment, you should be prepared for buyers to request some level of seller financing to bridge the gap between the bank loan and the total purchase price.

Seller Financing and Conventional Bank Loans

Conventional lenders prefer deals where the seller provides some financing. (Seller Financing will be explained in detail later in this chapter) This reduces the buyer's upfront cash requirement and serves as a risk-mitigation factor for the bank. If you as a seller are unwilling to finance part of the deal, it can raise red flags with lenders, causing them to question the stability of your business or your confidence in its future profitability.

How Seller Financing Fits Into Conventional Loans

- Many lenders limit their loan-to-value ratio to 70%-80% of the total purchase price. This means that if the business sells for $2 million, the bank may finance $1.4–$1.6 million. The remaining $400K–$600K must come from the buyer or from you (seller financing).

- A common structure is for the buyer to contribute 10%-20% of the total purchase price in cash, with the seller carrying 10%-20% in a promissory note to cover the gap.

- Unlike SBA loans, where seller financing is required to be on "standby" (meaning no payments for the first 2-3 years), conventional loans usually allow seller financing payments to begin immediately after closing.

Pros and Cons of Conventional Loans for Sellers

Like any financing method, conventional loans have both advantages and drawbacks from the seller's perspective.

Pros:

- **Potentially Faster Closing:** Conventional bank loans often have a shorter approval and closing process than SBA loans, which require extensive government oversight.

- **Larger Loan Amounts Possible:** If your business is valued over $5 million (the SBA cap), conventional loans may be necessary for a buyer to secure full financing.

- **Immediate Seller Financing Payments:** Unlike SBA loans, where seller-financed portions must be deferred for a period, payments on seller financing in conventional deals typically begin immediately.

Cons:

- **Higher Down Payment Requirement for Buyer:** This can reduce the number of qualified buyers who have the cash needed for the purchase.

- **Greater Likelihood of Seller Financing:** Since conventional loans cover less of the total price than SBA loans, you are more likely to be asked to finance a larger percentage of the deal.

- **More Varied Approval Processes:** Every bank has different underwriting standards, making it harder to predict whether a buyer will be approved.

What Sellers Should Consider

If your buyer is using a conventional loan, expect to negotiate some level of seller financing. This is not necessarily a negative - many sellers successfully structure financing agreements that provide them with additional interest income and a smoother transition. However, if you are resistant to seller financing, be prepared for lenders to scrutinize your reasons and question the long-term viability of the business.

Additionally, since conventional lenders do not have a government guarantee like the SBA, their underwriting process can vary widely from one bank to another. Buyers may approach multiple lenders before securing approval, which can extend the sale timeline.

Final Thoughts

Conventional loans are a solid option when SBA financing is unavailable or insufficient for the deal size. However, they require sellers to be more flexible, especially when it comes to seller financing. If your buyer is relying on conventional financing, be prepared to:

- **Be Patient** with the bank's approval process.

- **Provide Seller Financing** for 10%-20% of the deal.

- **Justify Your Valuation** to the lender, as they will conduct their own financial analysis before approving the loan.

With the right approach, conventional loans can be a useful tool for getting your business sold while ensuring a successful transition to the new owner.

Seller Financing

Many business owners enter the sale process hoping to receive full payment upfront, walk away with a briefcase full of cash, and start their next chapter without financial entanglements. While that's an ideal scenario, the reality is that 60–70% of small business acquisitions involve some level of seller financing. If you're unwilling to consider it, you may drastically reduce your pool of potential buyers and limit your ability to sell your business at the highest possible price.

What Is Seller Financing?

Seller financing means that you, as the seller, provide a loan to the buyer to cover part of the purchase price. Instead of receiving the full amount in cash at closing, you finance a certain percentage or the purchase price and receive scheduled payments, including interest, over a defined period. This arrangement can make your business more attractive to buyers who may not have enough capital to cover an entire down payment or have the ability to access full financing from traditional lenders.

Why You Should Consider Seller Financing

The biggest concern most sellers have about financing a portion of the deal is risk. How do you know you'll get paid? That's a valid concern, and while there's no way to guarantee full repayment, there are several measures you can take to protect yourself, which we will discuss further below.

Before we get to those measures, let's look at several reasons that seller financing is worth considering:

1. Expand Your Buyer Pool & Increase Demand

- Many qualified buyers can't secure full funding through banks or SBA loans.

- Offering seller financing makes your business more accessible, increasing the number of potential buyers.

- More competition among buyers leads to better sale prices and stronger deal terms.

2. Command a Higher Sale Price

- Buyers will often pay a premium for seller-financed deals because they may avoid some of the hurdles of traditional lenders.

- If you're flexible with financing, you may negotiate better overall terms.

Generate Ongoing Income with Interest

- Seller financing isn't just deferred payment, it's an investment opportunity.

- You can charge a competitive interest rate (currently 8-9%) and collect ongoing income, sometimes for years.

- This structured payout can provide financial stability, rather than a lump sum that may be taxed heavily.

Reduce Buyer Reliance on Banks

- If a buyer can't secure full financing from a bank, they may walk away.

- Seller financing fills the gap, making it easier to close the deal.

- You remain in control of the financing terms rather than relying on bank approvals.

Minimizing Risk in Seller Financing

Since you're acting as a lender, it's critical to structure the deal in a way that mitigates risk and ensures you get paid. Here's how:

1. Conduct Thorough Buyer Due Diligence

Before agreeing to seller financing, vet the buyer as a lender would:

- **Pull Their Credit Report** to check financial responsibility.

- **Verify Their Financial Statements** to ensure they can afford the payments.

- **Assess Their Business Experience** - do they have the skills to successfully operate your business?

- **Understand Their Assets** in case repayment issues arise.

2. Secure a Lien on the Business

Just as banks secure loans with collateral, you should place a lien on the business. This means:

- The buyer can't sell or take out new loans on the business without satisfying their debt to you.

- If the buyer defaults, you have legal rights to reclaim ownership.

- Liens protect you even if the business is resold.

3. Use a Promissory Note & Legal Agreements

Formal legal documentation is critical. The buyer should sign a promissory note that outlines:

- The loan amount and interest rate.

- The repayment schedule (monthly, quarterly, etc.).

- Consequences of missed payments.

- Default provisions that allow you to take legal action.

Your attorney should draft these agreements just as a bank would when lending money.

4. Include an Asset Reclaim Clause

A reclaim clause ensures that if the buyer stops making payments, you have the legal right to take back the business. While this isn't always ideal (if the business has been mismanaged, for example), it provides leverage to enforce payment.

5. Set Realistic Terms

- Typically, seller-financed portions range from 10% to 30% of the total sale price.

- Loan terms usually last 3 to 7 years.

- The buyer must make a reasonable down payment (e.g., 10-20%) to ensure they have "skin in the game."

- Interest rates should be set competitively but fairly to compensate for risk.

The Realities of Seller Financing

While seller financing carries some risk, structured correctly, it's a powerful tool to complete a profitable sale. In the vast majority of cases, buyers fulfill their obligations because:

- They've invested substantial money upfront and don't want to lose it.

- The business generates the cash flow needed to make payments.

- They understand that defaulting damages their reputation and financial future.

In the rare case that things go wrong, legal protections - including liens, asset claims, and collections agencies - can help recover funds.

A Real-World Example

In one transaction Marty handled, a seller financed 50% of the purchase price. After a year, the buyer realized they couldn't manage the business effectively. Instead of defaulting, they voluntarily transferred ownership to a new buyer, who resumed payments to the original seller.

The seller ultimately received the full payout - with interest - despite the first buyer's struggles.

While this won't happen in every case, having structured agreements and legal protections in place minimizes risk and maximizes your ability to recover funds.

Is Seller Financing Right for You?

If you want to sell your business faster, attract more buyers, and potentially secure a higher sale price, offering seller financing could be a smart move. However, you should:

- Conduct thorough due diligence on the buyer.

- Secure a lien on the business for protection.

- Have a detailed promissory note drafted by an attorney.

- Consider offering only a portion of the financing to limit exposure.

- Work with professionals to structure the safest possible deal.

Ultimately, seller financing isn't about whether you should offer it - it's about how to do it safely and profitably. When structured properly, it can lead to a smooth, lucrative transaction while giving the buyer the financial flexibility they need to close the deal now and succeed going forward.

Final Thought

Seller financing should be a tool that demonstrates your confidence in the buyer to other lenders, and provides a longer-term income stream. When planned strategically, it allows you to maximize your sale price, facilitate a successful deal, and secure a profitable return over time. If you approach it wisely, it can be a win-win for both you and the buyer.

Earnouts

An earnout is a financing mechanism that allows you to receive a portion of the sale price over time, based on the business meeting specific performance benchmarks. Unlike traditional seller financing, which operates as a structured loan, an earnout is directly tied to the future success of the business under its new owner. This structure is often used when a buyer is hesitant to pay your full asking price upfront, particularly if your valuation is based on projected - not historical - growth.

Why Buyers Use Earnouts

Buyers typically seek earnouts in two main scenarios:

1. When the Business is in Decline
If your business is experiencing a downturn, buyers may be uncertain about its future prospects. They may agree to pay a portion of your asking price upfront but will only release additional payments if revenue, profit, or other key performance indicators (KPIs) meet predefined targets.

2. When the Business is Growing Rapidly
If your business has shown strong growth, but much of its valuation is based on future projections rather than past performance, buyers may structure an earnout to ensure they are paying for actual - not just anticipated - success.

Earnouts offer a way to bridge the gap between what you believe your business is worth and what a buyer is willing to pay at closing. Instead of a buyer walking away from the deal, they may agree to your higher valuation, on the condition that the business performs as expected after the transition.

How Earnouts Work

Earnouts are structured based on specific milestones that the business must achieve post-sale. These milestones can include:

Revenue Benchmarks
Payments are released once the business reaches a certain revenue threshold.

Profit Targets
The new owner must generate a predetermined level of profit before releasing additional funds.

Time-Based Payouts
Earnout payments may be scheduled over a set period, such as quarterly or annually, provided the business remains operational and stable.

For example, if you sell your business for $2 million, a buyer may offer $1.5 million upfront and agree to pay the remaining $500,000 in increments over two years, provided the company maintains a certain level of profitability.

Passive vs. Active Earnouts

There are two main types of earnouts: passive and active.

Passive Earnouts
These are purely financial agreements. You are not involved in the business after the sale, and payments are based solely on whether the company meets its predefined financial targets.

Active Earnouts
These require your ongoing participation. In some cases, you may need to stay on board in some capacity for a defined period to ensure a smooth transition, maintain relationships with key clients, or continue contributing to revenue generation. Your payout is contingent on your efforts helping the company hit its targets.

The Role of a Salary in Active Earnouts

If your earnout agreement involves active participation, you may be offered a salary or consulting fee. This additional compensation helps ensure that you remain engaged in the business's success without solely relying on future earnout payments. In some cases, the earnout itself may be structured as your compensation, with the expectation that you actively work to help the company meet its goals.

Pros and Cons of Earnouts

Pros:

- **Higher Total Payout:** If your business achieves its projected growth, you can receive a higher sale price than an upfront cash-only deal.

- **Facilitates Deal Completion:** Earnouts can help bridge the valuation gap between you and the buyer, increasing the likelihood of closing a deal.

- **Provides Seller Confidence:** If you believe in your business's future success, an earnout allows you to profit from its continued growth.

Cons:

- **Risk of Non-Payment:** If the business fails to meet the agreed-upon benchmarks, you may not receive full payment.

- **Limited Control:** If you are not actively involved post-sale, you have no influence over business decisions that impact performance and your earnout payments.

- **Potential for Disputes:** Disagreements over financial reporting or goal-setting can arise, leading to delays or legal battles.

Structuring a Secure Earnout

If you agree to an earnout, take steps to protect yourself:

- **Clearly Define Performance Metrics:** Avoid vague language. Specify exact revenue or profit targets and how they will be measured.

- **Limit the Earnout Period:** The longer the earnout period, the greater the uncertainty. Keep it within 1-3 years if possible.

- **Ensure Transparency in Financial Reporting:** Require regular financial statements to verify business performance.

- **Include Protections Against Business Mismanagement:** Define conditions under which the earnout remains valid, ensuring that the buyer does not intentionally suppress revenue or shift profits to avoid payouts.

Is an Earnout Right for You?

Earnouts can be an effective tool in structuring a business sale, particularly when buyers and sellers have differing valuations. However, they come with inherent risks. If you are confident in your business's future potential and are comfortable with some degree of uncertainty, an earnout can help you maximize your total sale price. If, however, you want to walk away with guaranteed proceeds at closing, other financing structures may be a better fit.

Before agreeing to an earnout, consult with a qualified business broker, acquisitions advisor, or attorney to ensure the terms are fair, transparent, and enforceable. With careful planning, an earnout can be a powerful tool to bridge the gap between valuation expectations and secure a lucrative exit from your business.

ESOPs and MBOs

When considering a business sale, many owners focus on external buyers - competitors, private equity firms, or investors. However, one of the most viable and often overlooked buyer pools may be right under your roof: your employees or management team.

Two primary ways to transition ownership internally are Employee Stock Ownership Plans (ESOPs) and Management Buyouts (MBOs). Each option has its own advantages, challenges, and financial implications that you should fully understand before making a decision.

Employee Stock Ownership Plans (ESOPs): Selling to Your Team

An Employee Stock Ownership Plan (ESOP) allows you to sell your business to your employees, gradually or all at once, by forming a trust that purchases shares on their behalf. This can be a great option for business owners who want to reward their employees, maintain company culture, and provide a seamless transition.

How ESOPs Work

- A new ESOP trust is created, which buys your business shares using either bank financing or contributions from the business itself.

- Employees earn shares over time, usually as part of their compensation.

- When an employee leaves or retires, the ESOP buys back their shares, ensuring continued ownership transition.

Benefits of an ESOP Sale

- **Tax Advantages:** ESOPs can offer tax benefits for both the seller and the business. You may defer capital gains tax if the ESOP owns at least 30% of the company.

- **Business Continuity:** The company remains in the hands of those who know it best, ensuring cultural and operational stability.

- **Gradual Exit Option:** ESOPs allow you to phase out ownership over time rather than selling in one lump sum.

Challenges of an ESOP Sale

- **Complexity:** Setting up an ESOP is legally and financially intricate, often requiring valuation experts, attorneys, and third-party trustees.

- **Financing Risks:** Employees typically don't have the personal capital to buy a business outright, so funding often comes from business-generated profits or bank loans.

- **Regulatory Compliance:** ESOPs are governed by strict federal regulations, making ongoing administration a challenge.

For businesses with a strong, entrepreneurial-minded workforce, an ESOP can be a rewarding way to transition ownership while keeping the business in familiar hands.

Management Buyouts (MBOs): Selling to Key Leaders

A Management Buyout (MBO) is when one or more key members of your management team purchase your business. Unlike an ESOP, which distributes ownership broadly, an MBO concentrates ownership among a few select individuals who already play a leadership role in the company.

How MBOs Work

- A group of managers or a single leader arranges financing to buy the company.

- The purchase can be funded through SBA loans, conventional bank loans, or seller financing.

- The new owners assume full control, often with a structured transition period.

Benefits of an MBO Sale

- **Easier Transition:** Since your management team already knows the business, the transition is smoother and requires less training.

- **Higher Deal Success Rate:** Buyers with insider knowledge of the business's operations and financials are less likely to experience the setbacks that outside buyers might.

- **Flexible Financing:** Since managers may not have the full purchase price upfront, financing options like SBA-backed zero-down loans or seller-financed deals make it easier to structure a sale.

Challenges of an MBO Sale

- **Limited Buyer Pool:** Not all managers want to take on the risk of business ownership, which can narrow your list of potential buyers.

- **Seller Financing Expectations:** In many cases, you'll need to finance a portion of the sale yourself, deferring full payment over time.

- **Disruptions to Workplace Dynamics:** Employees may react emotionally to learning that their colleagues are now owners, creating potential workplace challenges.

If your management team has a strong desire to take over and run the business, an MBO can be a fast and effective exit strategy.

Getting Paid in an ESOP or MBO

How You Get Paid in an ESOP Sale

- The ESOP trust secures financing to purchase shares from you.

- Employees earn shares over time, and you get paid as shares are bought.

- Your exit may be structured over several years, allowing you to gradually receive payments and potentially defer capital gains tax.

How You Get Paid in an MBO Sale

- The management team secures financing, often through an SBA 7(a) loan, a conventional bank loan, or seller financing.

- If an SBA loan is used, you may need to finance 10% of the sale price yourself.

- The majority of your payment will come upfront, but a portion may be paid over time.

Which Option Is Right for You?

Choose an ESOP If:

- You want to reward employees with ownership.

- Your business has a strong, cohesive workforce.

- You're open to a structured, gradual payout.

- You're comfortable navigating the legal and financial complexities of ESOPs.

Choose an MBO If:

- You have key managers who are ready and willing to buy the business.

- You prefer a faster, more streamlined sale process.

- You want a more traditional transaction structure with SBA or bank financing.

- You're open to some level of seller financing to help facilitate the deal.

Final Thoughts: Ensuring a Smooth Internal Sale

Selling your business through an ESOP or an MBO can be a fulfilling way to transition ownership while maintaining company culture and rewarding those who have helped build the business. However, both methods require careful planning, legal structuring, and financial due diligence. If you're considering either of these paths, start the conversation early - especially with potential management buyers - to gauge their interest and ability to finance a deal.

In the end, whether you choose an ESOP or an MBO, the goal is the same: a successful transition that maximizes your financial return while ensuring the long-term success of the business you've built.

Section VI

Cashing Out
and
Living Large

What Does Cashing Out and Living Large Really Mean?

What will your life look like after you sell your business?

It's a question every owner must eventually face, and one that's far more powerful than it might first appear. Because, when you can paint a compelling picture of your life after the sale, you gain the motivation you need to do the work before the sale. This vision of your next chapter becomes your why, your driving force through the challenges of valuation, documentation, negotiation, and transition.

The fact of the matter is that cashing out and living large looks different for every owner. Some follow a classic retirement script. Others find new purpose in unexpected places. Some rediscover an old dream they nearly forgot. What matters most is that you begin envisioning your life after the sale - today.

Let us introduce you to three former owners who did exactly that.

From Rain to Sunshine: Patti's Move to Cabo

Patti had been running her Interior Design business in Oregon for over 20 years when she finally decided it was time to start taking the steps necessary to sell. Retirement had always been on the distant horizon, but now she saw it right in front of her. With Marty's help, she successfully exited - and then promptly left behind the cold and wet of the Pacific Northwest for a condo overlooking the ocean in Cabo San Lucas.

Today, Patti enjoys the weather, the food, the views, and the peace-of-mind that comes from knowing that the business she built is now allowing her to "live large" on her own terms. It's the quintessential "sunset chapter" many business owners dream of, and Patti earned every bit of it by preparing properly for her sale.

From Exit to Impact: Alex's Unexpected Pivot

Alex and his business partner didn't picture a beach retirement in their future. After selling their successful tech business, they initially planned to launch another startup more aligned with their passions. But then something unexpected happened.

Alex's grandfather fell victim to a financial scam, losing tens of thousands of dollars. That painful event sparked a new mission. The two founders used the capital from their sale to launch an entirely new company and foundation dedicated to protecting seniors from fraud. What began as a tech venture turned into a public service. Today, they speak at conferences, are recognized by government agencies, and have become national leaders in scam prevention. Selling their business didn't mean stepping away from meaningful work - it gave them the freedom to choose the kind of work that truly mattered to them.

Back to the Dream: The Auto Shop Owner's Aha Moment

Sometimes, your most attractive future may harken back to your past. One auto shop owner Marty worked with ran the biggest garage in town, with hundreds of five-star reviews and a bustling operation. He was making plenty of money, but he was also burning out. When asked why he wanted to sell, he couldn't quite put his finger on it, until recalling a distant memory lit him up like a light bulb.

"I want to restore classic cars," he told Marty. "That's what I wanted to do when I started this business!" But, somewhere along the way, the passion had faded into the grind. Now, by preparing for a profitable exit, he can return to that original dream - restoring vintage vehicles by hand, just a few per year, with less stress, more joy, and potentially even higher profits. He'll still be in the garage, but this time on his own terms. That's his version of living large.

What Does Post-Exit Life Look Like to You?

Each of these stories offers a glimpse into the possibilities waiting beyond the sale. Some are glamorous, others are grounded in purpose, and still others are rooted in personal rediscovery. There's no single right way to cash out and live large. There's only your way.

But here's the key: if you wait until after the sale to figure out what comes next, you may never get there at all.

Envisioning your future is more than a feel-good exercise, it's a powerful motivator that can help you push through the sometimes difficult work of preparing your business for sale. It helps you focus, make better decisions, and stay committed through the ups and downs of the sale process.

So before we dive into the nuts and bolts of life after your exit, we invite you to ask yourself: What does your version of living large look like? And how can we help you make it real?

Your Personal Journey to Cashing Out and Living Large

Selling your business is not just a financial transaction—it's a life transition. For many business owners, the sale of their business represents the culmination of decades of hard work, risk-taking, and perseverance. But what happens after the deal closes? How do you ensure that the next chapter of your life is as fulfilling, meaningful, and rewarding as your years of business ownership?

The answer lies in intentional planning, financial wisdom, and emotional preparation. In this section, we will explore how to transition from business owner to financially secure and personally fulfilled retiree or next-phase entrepreneur. We will also address the psychological and emotional challenges of letting go, as discussed in Frank's interviews with Jerome Myers, author of Exit to Excellence, and psychotherapist Diana Gibb.

More Than a Paycheck: Your Business is Part of Your Identity

Business owners do not just build companies, they build identities, relationships, and legacies. Your business is an extension of who you are. It has been the source of your financial success, your purpose, and your daily routine for years, maybe decades. That's why selling is not just about money; it's about what comes next and who you are after the sale.

As Jerome Myers points out in Exit to Excellence, many business owners feel unprepared for life after selling because they have not built a vision for what they want their post-business life to look like. Instead, they are left feeling unmoored, disconnected, and unsure of their purpose.

Diana Gibb has seen this play out in her work as a psychotherapist. She describes how major life transitions - whether retirement, the loss of a loved one, or a career change - can be emotionally jarring. Business owners may struggle with anxiety, regret, or even depression after exiting their business, especially if they have not taken proactive steps to mentally and emotionally prepare.

The key takeaway? Do not wait until after the sale to figure out what's next. You need a plan, not just for selling your business, but for what you will do with your life afterward.

Turning a Lump Sum Into Long-Term Wealth

If you have positioned your business properly, the sale should result in a significant financial windfall. But "having" money and "managing" money are two very different things. Many business owners are experts at building a business but novices at personal wealth management.

Consider These Key Financial Steps Post-Sale:

- **Assemble Your Wealth Management Team:** Just as you needed an exit team to sell your business, you now need financial advisors, tax strategists, and estate planners to help protect and grow your wealth.

- **Understand the Tax Implications:** How much of your sale proceeds will you actually keep? Proper tax planning can significantly impact your net worth.

- **Develop a Long-Term Investment Strategy:** Whether you plan to live off the interest, invest in real estate, or fund new ventures, you need a structured plan to preserve and grow your wealth.

- **Don't Make Rash Spending Decisions:** Many sellers feel "cash rich" after a sale and make impulsive purchases - vacation homes, luxury cars, risky investments - that they later regret. Take time to breathe and strategize before making any major financial commitments. We go into this topic in greater detail in the next chapter, 15 Common Mistakes and How to Avoid Them.

Finding Purpose and Avoiding "Seller's Remorse"

Some business owners have clear post-exit plans, they want to travel, spend more time with family, or start a new venture. But others struggle with a loss of identity after selling.

Jerome Myers emphasizes that many entrepreneurs thrive on the challenges and excitement of business ownership. The sudden loss of structure, goals, and daily engagement can lead to a feeling of aimlessness or regret.

Strategic Options for Fulfillment After Selling:

- **Start a New Venture (If You Want To):** Just because you sold one business doesn't mean you can't start another, this time with more freedom and capital. Did you know that Harlan Sanders franchised his first Kentucky Fried Chicken (KFC) at age 65?

- **Consult, Mentor, or Invest:** Many former business owners find meaning by mentoring other entrepreneurs, serving on advisory boards, or becoming investors in new startups.

- **Give Back:** Philanthropy, non-profits, and impact-driven projects can provide a sense of purpose and legacy.

- **Pursue Interests Beyond Business:** What have you always wanted to do but never had time for? Travel, hobbies, and passion projects can bring new meaning to your life after selling.

Living Large - On Your Own Terms

For years, your definition of success was tied to the growth and profitability of your business. Now, success is about how you enjoy your time, financial freedom, and personal fulfillment.

The best post-sale outcomes come from intentionality. Don't just sell your business, design your future.

Key Takeaways: What You Need to Do Before and After Selling

- **Prepare For The Emotional Transition:** Selling your business is a major life change, and you need a clear plan for what comes next.

- **Develop A Financial Strategy:** Work with professionals to ensure long-term security and intelligent wealth management.

- **Find New Sources Of Fulfillment:** Whether it's mentoring, philanthropy, or launching another venture, plan for purpose beyond the sale.

- **Enjoy Your Success, But With Intention:** This is your opportunity to live life on your terms. Make it count.

Final Thought: You Are in Control

Selling your business is not the end of the road - it's the start of a new journey. With the right preparation, mindset, and planning, you can turn this transition into the most exciting and fulfilling chapter of your life.

You've built something great. Now it's time to go out and LIVE LARGE!

15 Common Post-Exit Mistakes and How to Avoid Them

As we have said many times throughout this book, exiting from your business is not the end of the process, it is the beginning of a new life filled with time freedom and financial security. But that wonderful new life won't last very long if you haven't prepared in advance to manage your financial windfall and avoid the mistakes that we so frequently see owners make post-exit.

Below is a top-level list of fifteen common mistakes business owners often make after selling their businesses, along with preparatory steps to avoid those pitfalls. For a more comprehensive deep-dive into these issues, enroll in our course and/or be on the lookout for our live educational events.

1. Impulsive Spending

Mistake: Engaging in lavish expenditures on luxury items, travel, or significant lifestyle upgrades immediately after receiving the sale proceeds.

Preparation: Implement a cooling-off period to allow for thoughtful financial planning. Develop a comprehensive financial plan that aligns with long-term goals before making substantial purchases.

2. Neglecting Tax Planning

Mistake: Underestimating or overlooking the tax obligations associated with the sale, leading to unexpected liabilities.

Preparation: Consult with tax professionals well in advance of the sale to understand potential tax implications and strategies to minimize liabilities, such as structuring the sale appropriately or utilizing tax deferral options.

3. Lack of Investment Strategy

Mistake: Failing to develop a strategy for investing the sale proceeds, resulting in suboptimal growth or unnecessary risk exposure.

Preparation: Work with a financial advisor to create an investment plan tailored to your risk tolerance, time horizon, and financial objectives, ensuring diversification and alignment with your future income needs.

4. Mixing Personal and Business Finances

Mistake: Continuing to intertwine personal and business finances post-sale, leading to accounting complications and potential legal issues.

Preparation: Establish clear boundaries by separating personal and business accounts, and ensure all financial transactions are appropriately categorized and documented.

5. Ignoring Cash Flow Management

Mistake: Overlooking the importance of managing cash flow, which can lead to liquidity issues despite having substantial assets.

Preparation: Develop a detailed budget that accounts for regular expenses, taxes, and planned investments to maintain adequate liquidity and avoid financial strain.

6. Overestimating Financial Resources

Mistake: Assuming the sale proceeds will sustain any level of spending indefinitely, without considering longevity and inflation.

Preparation: Conduct a thorough analysis of your financial needs over time, factoring in life expectancy, healthcare costs, and inflation, to ensure sustainable withdrawals from your assets.

7. Failing to Pay Off High-Interest Debt

Mistake: Keeping high-interest debts while holding onto cash, resulting in unnecessary interest expenses.

Preparation: Prioritize paying off high-interest debts to reduce financial liabilities and improve net worth.

8. Not Establishing an Emergency Fund

Mistake: Investing all proceeds without setting aside liquid funds for unforeseen expenses or emergencies.

Preparation: Allocate a portion of the proceeds to an easily accessible emergency fund covering 6-12 months of living expenses.

9. Neglecting Estate Planning

Mistake: Failing to update or establish an estate plan, potentially causing complications for heirs and unintended distribution of assets.

Preparation: Work with an estate planning attorney to draft or revise wills, trusts, and beneficiary designations to reflect your current wishes and maximize tax efficiencies.

10. Overlooking Insurance Needs

Mistake: Allowing insurance policies to lapse or not reassessing coverage needs, exposing oneself to unforeseen risks.

Preparation: Review and update insurance policies, including health, life, and liability insurance, to ensure adequate coverage in your new financial situation.

11. Succumbing to Lifestyle Inflation

Mistake: Gradually increasing lifestyle expenses to match your new wealth, which can erode financial gains over time.

Preparation: Maintain disciplined spending habits and adhere to a budget that supports long-term financial goals without unnecessary lifestyle inflation.

12. Not Seeking Professional Financial Advice

Mistake: Attempting to manage newfound wealth without professional guidance, leading to potential missteps and missed opportunities.

Preparation: Assemble a team of trusted financial professionals, including a financial advisor, tax consultant, and estate planner, to provide comprehensive guidance tailored to your situation.

13. Making Hasty Investment Decisions

Mistake: Quickly investing large sums into unfamiliar or high-risk ventures without adequate due diligence.

Preparation: Take time to thoroughly research investment opportunities and consider starting with a conservative approach before committing to more aggressive strategies.

14. Failing to Plan for Retirement

Mistake: Assuming the sale proceeds will be sufficient for retirement without proper planning, potentially leading to shortfalls in later years.

Preparation: Develop a detailed retirement plan that includes projected expenses, income sources, and investment strategies to ensure financial security throughout retirement.

15. Overlooking Charitable Giving Strategies

Mistake: Neglecting to incorporate charitable contributions into financial planning, missing out on potential tax benefits and philanthropic goals.

Preparation: Explore charitable giving options, such as donor-advised funds or charitable trusts, to fulfill philanthropic objectives while optimizing tax advantages.

Final Thought

By proactively addressing these areas and engaging in thorough planning with qualified professionals, you can effectively manage the financial windfall from selling your business and secure your long-term financial well-being.

Next Steps
and
Additional Resources

Here's What to Do Next

Congratulations on completing this book! Below is a list of next steps and additional resources we encourage you to engage with.

Register Your Book Purchase

We greatly appreciate your purchase of our book and we'd like to get to know you better! Just go to BoomerSellsTheBusiness.com and click on the "Register Your Book" link on the homepage. That will give you instant access to our proprietary checklist, Seven Steps to Sale-Ready Condition that you can print out and reference as you prepare your business for sale.

Complete the Companion Workbook

Our Companion Workbook (available on Amazon) is a step-by-step guide to taking all the actions described in this book. Buy the Workbook, follow the instructions, complete the checklists, fill in the forms and Get 'er Done!

Join Our Facebook Community

Boomer Sells The Business is more than a book or a course, Boomer Sells The Business is a movement. And the best way to become a part of that movement is as a member of our Facebook community. Just type "Boomer Sells The Business" into the Facebook search bar and click "Join" when you find it. Then feel free to ask questions of the group, post success stories, ask for referrals - you name it!

Subscribe to Our Email Newsletter

Every week we publish an email newsletter containing resources, success stories, tips and tricks, and information about our upcoming live events - both online and in-person. If you've already registered your book, you're on the email distribution list. If not, click the "Newsletter" link on the homepage at BoomerSellsTheBusiness.com and sign up.

Enroll in Our Online MasterClass

If you're looking for more detailed help in preparing your business for sale, but aren't ready to sign up for monthly coaching calls, we encourage you to enroll in the Boomer Sells The Business online MasterClass. Click the "MasterClass" link on the homepage of BoomerSellsTheBusiness.com to learn more about what the course includes and how to enroll to get instant access.

Attend Our In-Person and Online Educational Events

Marty and Frank host frequent online and in-person educational events. If you are on our email list you will receive invitations to each event. If you're not on our list, click the "Newsletter" link on the homepage at BoomerSellsTheBusiness.com and sign up.

Have Marty Estimate the Value of Your Business

Wonder what your business is worth today and what steps you need to take to get it to where you want it to be? Scan the QR Code below and then fill out the application form to see if you qualify for a $2,000 preliminary valuation by Marty.

Alternatively, click the "MasterClass" link on the homepage of BoomerSellsTheBusiness.com and enroll. Every student in our online MasterClass receives a complimentary call with Marty where, among other insights, he will give you his estimate of the current value of your business in the marketplace.

BOOMER SELLS THE BUSINESS

A Step-by-Step Guide to Cashing Out & Living Large

FRANK FELKER | MARTY M FAHNCKE

POWER HOUSE PUBLISHING

ALEXANDRIA
VIRGINIA